OVID'S HEROINES

Clare Pollard was born in Bolton in 1978 and lives in London. She has published five collections with Bloodaxe: *The Heavy-Petting Zoo* (1998), which she wrote while still at school, *Bedtime* (2002); *Look, Clare! Look!* (2005); *Changeling* (2011), a Poetry Book Society Recommendation; and Incarnation (2017). Her translation *Ovid's Heroines* was published by Bloodaxe in 2013. Her play *The Weather* (Faber, 2004) premièred at the Royal Court Theatre. She works as an editor, broadcaster and teacher. Her documentary for radio, *My Male Muse* (2007), was a Radio 4 Pick of the Year. She is co-editor, with James Byrne, of *Voice Recognition: 21 Poets for the 21st Century* (Bloodaxe Books, 2009), and translator (with Maxamed Xasan 'Alto' and Said Jama Hussein) of Asha Lul Mohamud Yusuf's *The Sea-Migrations* (Somali title: *Tahriib*), published by Bloodaxe Books in 2017 with The Poetry Translation Centre. In 2017 she took over the editorship of *Modern Poetry in Translation*. Her non-fiction book *Fierce Bad Rabbits: The Tales Behind our Picture Books* was published by Fig Tree in 2019.

CLARE POLLARD

OVID'S HEROINES

BLOODAXE BOOKS

First published 2013 by
Bloodaxe Books Ltd,
Eastburn,
South Park,
Hexham,
Northumberland NE46 1BS.

www.bloodaxebooks.com
For further information about Bloodaxe titles
please visit our website or write to
the above address for a catalogue.

Supported by
**ARTS COUNCIL
ENGLAND**

COVER PHOTOGRAPH

Lee Miller, in Jean Cocteau's film *The Blood of a Poet*
by Man Ray (1930)
© Man Ray Trust / ADAGP, BI, Paris 2013
with kind permission from M. Pierre Bergé,
président of the Comité Jean Cocteau

Cover design: Neil Astley & Pamela Robertson-Pearce.

Map of Ovid's world (page 8): Richard Henson

This is a digital reprint of the 2013 Bloodaxe Books edition.

For Matthew

Contents

OVID'S WORLD

ROME CARTHAGE GREEK ISLANDS TOMIS COLCHIS

ATHENS LEMNOS TROY THRACE LESBOS

CORINTH PHYLACE ITHACA

SPARTA MYCENAE CRETE DIA (NAXOS) LYDIA

8

INTRODUCTION

I

When I was working on this new version of Ovid's *Heroides*, I was invited with my husband to the island of Santorini for the wedding of some friends. We flew into Athens to get the boat, and also spent a few days on Amorgos. I took Richard Lattimore's translation of *The Iliad* to read on the vast ferries as they churned past schools of dolphins.

It was a wonderful trip. The wedding was outside, in a white-washed courtyard, and then we feasted and danced under the moon, drinking glasses of the golden local wine. We visited a volcano, bathed in belching sulphur pools, and then were schlepped up a hill by donkeys. The sea was the most clear and pale-green I have ever seen. One day we swam to a beach through a narrow, glowing cave; on another we saw a fat, black eel. On Amorgos there were white villages with windmills; rocky outcrops that smelt of wild thyme.

The ferries, though, were a nightmare. The distances between the islands were much further than I'd imagined, and there were strikes. No one knew when they were going to go. Hours were spent on the phone, on hold to travel agents, hearing conflicting stories, or else sat waiting on the boiling concrete docks. As another ferry left without us on it and, perched on my backpack, I read of Homer's 'baleful battle' between godlike men, I would think of the women they had left behind. Often just-married, they had been immediately abandoned, and left standing on the beaches, or the cliffs, or the harbour, watching their men go off to Troy. Grieving. Impotent. Stuck, stuck, stuck.

II

The year before, coincidentally, I had been in Rome for another wedding (I was thirty and going to a lot of weddings), reading the *Heroides* for the first time. I always try to pick my reading matter to match my location, and I had with me Ovid's *The Art of Love*, translated by James Michie, as well as a battered old copy of George Showerman's 1914 Loeb translation of the *Heroides*, borrowed from a library. The only Ovid I had read before was Ted Hughes' version of the *Metamorphoses*, and so I was surprised and charmed by James Michie's rendering of Ovid's voice in *The Art of Love* – how dry and modern it was. Born in 43 BC, Ovid was sent to Rome as a boy to study, and lived in the city until Augustus sent him into exile in 8 AD to Tomis by the Black Sea (for what seems to have been his involvement or complicity in some scandal, although historians have never quite solved the mystery). For most of his life, Ovid was very much a Roman poet, so I could almost glimpse him as I strolled through the Forum or by the Circus Maximus (as he noted, at the Circus you could: 'sit as close to a girl as you please, / so make the most of touching thighs and knees').

Then I started to read the *Heroides*, and as I began to realise what it actually was – a retelling of the Greek myths from the perspective of the women (Phaedra was there, and Medea, and Penelope) I got a feverish, vertigo-feeling. That mixture of excitement and panic every writer feels when they have a brilliant idea. The prose translation had dated, but behind the archaisms I could glimpse something astonishing. I had to write a new version of this! How had I never heard of this book before?

The wedding ceremony was Catholic and in Latin – impenetrable to me, of course, my state school in Bolton not teaching the classics, but I did not let this detail put me off my new project. The party afterwards was on a nearby beach. This is life, I thought to myself, prosecco in hand, as candles wobbled in the sea breeze and the newlyweds gazed at each other. *It's about love.* And this, it seems to me, is why the *Heroides* is a great book. It takes huge narratives of nationhood, war, death, myth and religion, but it puts love at the centre. Because it may sound a little cheesy but in the end love, for most of us, is what matters. (I'm at a wedding, drinking prosecco, okay? Such observations are allowed.)

III

Yet the sober truth is that for this reason the *Heroides* has often been dismissed. By putting love at its heart, it has been seen as trivialising and domesticating great legends, with the criticism often smacking slightly of misogyny – the critic Brooks Otis talks of: 'the wearisome complaint of the reft maiden, the monotonous iteration of her woes', whilst Howard Jacobson moans of 'grating and carping women'. Irritatingly, whenever the heroines do show strength and humour, this is also condemned. L.P. Wilkinson sneeringly notes that: 'The heroines are not too miserable to make puns.' The implication is that any wit in the voices is just Ovid showing his face through the mask, unable to sustain character. Because, obviously, women are never ironic.

Heroides is a radical collection of poems. It is a daring act of literary transvestism. It is an attempt to modernise and revitalise well-worn myths. Its narrators' stories are deeply subjective, partial and often unreliable, with this highlighted by telling the same stories from different perspectives. It has been called both the first book of dramatic monologues and the first of epistolary fiction. For a long time, it was Ovid's most loved and influential text, its impact visible in Chaucer's 'The Legend of the Good Women', Dante, Marlowe, Shakespeare, Donne. It was translated by Dryden and Pope...

Yet on the dispiriting days I spent in the British Library trawling essays about the *Heroides*, it seemed like I'd made a mistake and was wasting my time on a minor text. Mean-spirited critics repeatedly talked of Ovid's failure or his manipulative presence – usually proving their points with their own flat-footed translations – with Florence Verducci claiming that 'even the most closely reasoned and dispassionate argument for the poetic merit of Ovid's collection will whisper of the marketplace, the boutique for overpriced and at best second-rate antiquities.'

'This is OVID!' I wanted to shout. 'He's simultaneously inventing about four genres! Have some *respect*!!'

Of course, there are flaws. I am inclined to think no work of real genius is ever without flaws – anyone staking out entirely new territory is bound to make mistakes as they feel their way. Yes, as Pope said, Ovid Romanizes his Greeks, but historical realism is a bit much to ask for in the territory of myth (Shakespeare put Theseus and Hippolyta next to some very English woods). Sappho's letter now strikes us as the weakest of the *Heroides*, because we know her work and Ovid's impersonation seems so far off the mark. However, read it as the voice of a lyric love poet (like Ovid) who has played the field and is now growing old (like Ovid) and it becomes much more enjoyable – a kind of self-portrait in drag. For Ovid, as for Virginia Woolf, a portrait of the creative mind is one of the 'androgynous mind'.

11

Elsewhere there is indeed some melodrama and silliness – the gossip about Hercules dressing as a woman, or Cassandra predicting that a Greek Cow will ruin Oenone's life – but this is done knowingly. In these episodes Ovid is having fun; tipping into what we might almost call camp. These passionate Mediterranean women remind me of a Pedro Almodóvar film, or a scrap of Italian soap-opera glimpsed late at night, whilst flicking through porn and game-shows in a Venetian hotel.

It's also true that Ovid can be repetitive, but the repetitions are often deliberate and, in fact, part of the poetry – both its music and its wider structure. Each of these women is essentially put in the same position – backed into a trap by their gender; unable to act; expected to passively wait for the men, who may or may not come to save them. As an illustration of the sheer frustration of gender roles, the accumulative effect of the *Heroides* is to fill you with rage and heartbreak. Yet there is still huge variety in their stories. And in the letters they exercise the power they do have: the power of words.

The motives behind each letter are, in fact, very different indeed, as are the strategies they use to escape from their predicaments – some heroic, some cowardly. The letters are attempts to seduce, plead, threaten, comfort or curse. They range from the anxious letters of a worried wife to vengeful suicide-notes. Deianira, a kind of classical WAG, tries to deal with her husband Hercules' fame; a slave attempts to keep her dignity whilst being used as a pawn in the Trojan War; a queen begs her husband's son for sex. They articulate love in all its beautiful, messy, stupid complexity.

They are likely to put a modern reader in mind of other texts that retell history from a woman's perspective. But the fact that these were written by a *man* over *2000 years ago* is astonishing. It would be absurd to claim Ovid as some proto-feminist, and he is not sympathetic to all his personae – some are immature, or vain, or evil – but as a sustained act of empathy, the *Heroides* is remarkable. These are three-dimensional women, thinking aloud; displaying intelligence, dazzling rhetoric, self-deprecating humour or cruel calculation. If they put love before everything else, it is not because they are small-minded, but rather because Ovid does too.

IV

Luckily, when I began work I hadn't yet read the critics, so had no doubts. The first draft of the translation I did fairly quickly, with a sense of euphoria. I worked from the Loeb and another old translation by Harold Cannon, with a dictionary at my side. I felt like an archeologist, brushing the soil and dust off each line, holding it up to the daylight and discovering something beautiful. Even the title came up rather brilliantly as Heroines.

I should probably mention that early on I had to make a decision about form. Ovid writes in elegiac couplets, and in English translators often attempt to echo this by using some kind of metrical couplet. However, an attempt to impose such strict form throughout a long translation necessarily involves many other compromises with the material – in translations of the *Heroides*, particularly, it often seems to mean a loss of concision and suppleness of tone. If heroic couplets are chosen, it can also create a rather eighteenth-century atmosphere, when I wanted to show readers that this text is startlingly modern. I therefore decided to follow Ted Hughes' example and choose free verse, allowing me to explore other aspects of Ovid's poetry – the pacing, the hypnotic repetitions, the tragi-comic shifts, the immediacy of the voices.

For those who want a scholarly translation, I would recommend Harold Isbell's for Penguin Classics. He's the one translator I've found who doesn't seem to be apologising for Ovid's text, but actually likes it (fairly crucial, I think) and I found his notes very useful. It also contains the disputed *Double Heroides*, which were probably written much later, where the male lovers also correspond – Leander to Hero, Paris to Helen – and which I decided, because of their separateness, not to include here. Though I ended up doing considerable research between drafts, this is ultimately a poet's version, written for pleasure. I hope people will read it in Rome's cafés after lunch, sipping a *caffè* as their *saltimbocca* is cleared away and water plays in a fountain; or perhaps by a pool in Crete under the scalding Greek sun. Ovid's *Heroides* was historically one of his most popular texts: it deserves to be so again.

Marcus loves Spendusa

Serena hates Isidore

Sarra, you're not acting very nicely, leaving me all alone

Restitutus has deceived many girls many times

I have f_____ many girls here

I came here, I f_____, I went home

Let him who loves, prosper. Let him who loves not, perish.
And let him who forbids love to others perish twice over.

Graffiti from Pompeii, trans. Jo-Ann Shelton

14

I: Penelope to Ulysses

With this letter, Ovid puts a different perspective on Homer's *The Odyssey*. The Trojan War has long been over, but the Greek war-hero Ulysses has not returned to his wife Penelope in Ithaca. Whilst those who have read Homer will know this is because he has been waylaid by obstacles that include Gods, monsters, weather and the sorceress Circe, Penelope has heard nothing. Their son Telemachus has just returned from a fruitless trip to Pylos, where he was trying to find out what has happened to his father and was almost killed. Penelope is losing patience with both Ulysses himself and the suitors who in his absence are after her hand in marriage (and her wealth).

In many versions of the story, Penelope manages to stall the suitors by saying she will only decide between them once she has finished weaving a shroud for her father-in-law Laertes, then un-ravelling it at night – in Ovid's retelling though, this idea is only subtly alluded to.

¶

Dear Ulysses,

you're late.

Don't worry about answering, just come home.
The enemy of Grecian wives has fallen,
but, honestly, Troy wasn't worth it.

If only Paris had drowned
in some storm when he was heading for Sparta,
I wouldn't lie frigid in my bed
or have to moan of tedious days
or pass my nights like some poor widow
at the loom's dull web.

I mean, I know love makes me anxious
and my nightmares were excessive –
lurid scenarios; Trojans singling you out etc.
Hector's name made me ashen.
When I heard he'd killed Antilochus,
I was a nervous mess.
Then Patroclus died, in borrowed armour,
so even cunning couldn't guarantee success…
Each time Greek blood warmed spears
I was flooded with fear.

But someone must look out for couples:
Troy burnt and you survived.
Now soldiers slur victory songs;
smoke coils from altars laid with souvenirs;
admiration makes old men babble
as girls hang on tales from lovers' lips.

The other night, one man mapped battles
in spilt wine, lightly tracing Troy:
'The river was here; Priam's palace,
Achilles' tent, then Hector's corpse…'

I sent our son to find you – he got the story:
how you, full of your daring – not caring about us –
stole into the Trojan camp at night
and just two of you slaughtered hundreds.
Sounds typically cautious and thoughtful.
Until I heard you'd ridden back, my heart
reared with fear at every word.

Anyway, you've razed Troy, but what does it matter
to me it's been levelled?
I remain as I was while it remained –
alone.

It's like for others Troy's destroyed
but for me it stands,
though turned to farming land
where fields of corn lift from blood-plump earth.
The ploughshare's blade disturbs half-buried bones;
weeds smother palaces.
You won, but you're not here. I don't know why,
or where in the world you are.

I quiz each ship arriving at our port.
I push letters in their hands
in case your courses cross.
We sent word to Nestor's land,
but his reply was 'nothing's sure';
to Sparta too, but they could tell us nothing true.

Where are you?
If only I'd not prayed for victory!
At least I'd know where you were and war would be my only fear,
and I wouldn't be the only one worried.
Now there's just this uneasiness –
I fret without focus.

I blame the dangers of islands or seas
when, for all my silly fears,
you might just be snared by some exotic tart –
you're male, after all.

You might be saying how provincial I am:
'Domestic goddess; good with wool...'
I hope I'm wrong and this is just a wisp of fancy –
that you haven't chosen not to come back.

As for me, my father wants me to wed again,
criticises me for taking too long.
But let him witter! I'm yours:
I'm Ulysses' wife.
My loyalty wins us some time
but there are *lots* of local suitors: a lecherous pack.
In your own hall they're masters, with no one to say no –
I have to say they're ruining your things.

I won't bore you with detail –
the nastiness and grasping paws,
all those guzzling in your absence
from cupboards you fought to fill –
but there are only the three of us, unused to fighting:
your father, myself and Telemachus, our boy.
Recently, they meant to murder him.
(God, I pray our family dies in the right order –
that he's the one to close my eyes, and yours.)

Our allies are an ancient nurse, the cowherd
and the man who keeps the pigs!
Your father can't hold a weapon,
let alone the realm amidst our enemies;
Telemachus will grow stronger – so long as he lives –
but only if his father guides him.

I haven't strength to drive these bastards from our halls.

Do you hurry, my haven, my refuge?
You have – let's pray you keep – a son
who's vulnerable, who needs you.
Think of your father too –
he feels he can't die until you're here...

As for myself, I was a young girl when you went away,
but you'll come back to a fully-grown woman.

II: Phyllis to Demophoon

Phyllis is a princess in Thrace (a region which mainly overlaps with contemporary Bulgaria, along with parts of north-eastern Greece and Turkey). Demophoon is the son of Theseus (a recurring figure of male cruelty in *Heroines*). On his return journey from the Trojan War, Demophoon accepts Phyllis' hospitality in Thrace, falls in love with her and takes her virginity. Then, after making great promises, he leaves on urgent business and does not return. In this letter to him, she has begun to accept that, for all her patient waiting, he might not be coming back.

There is an interesting coda to this letter, which is essentially a suicide note. In some versions of the tale, Phyllis metamorphoses into an almond tree after her death. When Demophoon returns and embraces the tree in grief, its branches burst into blossom.

¶

You know the mountain we visited?
I'm stood there, crying.
The promised day has passed and you're not here.

You swore before the moon was full
the shores would feel your anchor
but four moons waned and waxed
and the tide brings no ships from Attica.

If you've counted the days
– as lovers count days –
you'll know I don't complain too soon.
Hope left reluctantly,
even now, I'm loath to think you wrong.

I deceived myself to defend you.
I cursed weather for wracking your sails;
Theseus for holding you back.
Your boat was burst or swallowed.
I lit incense, dropped to knees (oh
you bad, bad man) to pray.
When sky and sea were still, I told myself:
'He's on his way'; concocted obstacles.

But *you* delay,
neither the gods you swore upon or my love bring you back.
You gave your sails and words to air;
sails don't come, your promise fails.

Apart from lovingly stupidly, what have I done?
My fault was to want.
My only crime is that I took you for myself,
but I thought you'd be pleased.

Where are your pledges now,
your lying lips?

Where's your proposal; that vow about forever?
You swore by the tempest-tossed sea;
by your grandfather who calms those waves
(if he's not fiction too.)
You swore by my torturer, Venus;
by Juno, who watches bridal beds,
by mystic rites...
If all those vexed gods took vengeance
you could not pay in one life.

Yes and, like a fool, I repaired your ship's keel,
by which you left me!
I gave you oars by which you fled:
I self-harm.

I trusted your wheedling words – your many –
I trusted your lineage,
I trusted your tears – can these be feigned too?
Do they also swindle, pouring to order?
What was the point of making so many vows?
By just one word of any one, however slight, I would have been
          undone.

I don't regret sheltering you,
but that should have been all.
I'm ashamed I played hostess in the bedroom;
pushed my body to yours.

I wish I'd died the night before.
I wish I'd died a virgin.
To beguile a gullible girl
is a cheap victory.
To hoax a smitten woman
is not an achievement.

Your statue should be in your city's square
beside your father's, recording his mighty triumphs:
the Minotaur, Thebes brought low in war,
the flight of Centaurs.

After this, under your image, these words:

He betrayed a woman's love whilst her guest.

Just one of your father's deeds inspired you:
deserting Ariadne.
You are heir to his slyness, you crook.
Of course, Ariadne found a better match
in Bacchus' chariot, pulled by tigers –
but I will not be wed.
I took a stranger to my bed.

They're saying: 'Let her go to Athens,
we'll find someone else to rule Thrace –
it's for the best.'
Damn those who measure deeds by results!
Yet, if our seas swirled beneath your oar,
I would be thought wise as a lover; a ruler.
But no – it's impossible.
My palace won't feel your presence,
you won't bathe tired bones in our bays.

I can't help picturing you the day you left,
your ships eager in the harbour.
You dared to hold me, arms wrapped tight around my neck,
and your lips were kissing mine
and your tears mixed with mine
and you complained about fine weather
and as you left me, you said:
'Phyllis, expect your Demophoon.'

And what can I expect, when you never mean to see me again?
Am I to wait for a ship that won't return?
And yet I do wait. Oh return –
be here late, not never.

Why do I bother?
You're wed to someone else by now.
You've probably forgotten me.

You'd probably ask: who's Phyllis?
I'm the woman who welcomed you when you were lost,
heaped you with gifts and would have given more.
I offered you a wide, wide realm.

Ignoring omens, I gave you my innocence,
your hand untying; seeking secret parts.

Do you think the Furies watched?
There was a howl; the croaks of owls;
a writhing of snakes.
Light like the light in a tomb...

And yet I pace the stony beach
to scan the sea when I see it.
Whether the soil is loose with warmth or constellations glare
          coldly,
I'm always watching wind sweep the straits.
When I see far sails
I think my wish has been answered
and rush to the water
and run into the spume.
When they get nearer, my strength ebbs.
I slump into my maid's arms.

There is a path, curled in a sickle shape,
that ends in high cliffs.
I have been thinking about throwing myself from them.
Since you're faithless, I will –
let the waves carry me to you,
let my broken body float to your feet.
You might at least say:
'She shouldn't have.'

Poison's my thirst; I hanker for swords
to pierce my chest to spurt out blood.
Since your arms wrapped tight around my neck,
I've longed to put it in a noose.

My heart is fixed on death: it is a kind of purity.
Choosing the method's all that's left.
On my tomb they'll inscribe my story.
By this suicide note, you'll be known.

III: Briseis to Achilles

Briseis is not a well developed character in Homer's *Iliad*, but she is important. At the beginning of the Trojan War, her family are slaughtered at Lyrnessus and she is taken by the Greek's greatest warrior, Achilles, as a prize of war – a concubine. Achilles argues with Agamemnon, who then takes Briseis. After this Achilles retires from combat to sulk in his tent, refusing to fight. It is this refusal that arguably leads to his dear friend Patroclus' death, and the thirst for vengeance which ends in the slaughter of Hector.

This letter brilliantly fleshes out Briseis into a complex woman, torn between love and tactics. Full of contradictions, she is an articulate barbarian; a powerless *femme fatale*; a fiercely proud slave who knows her only hope is plead.

¶

This letter you are reading is from Briseis:
abducted, a barbarian, barely able to write Greek.
The smears are tears.
I hope them strong as words.

My master, my beloved,
if I'm allowed a brief complaint, I'll complain.
That I was given up, so easily, when Agamemnon demanded
is not your fault – yet is.
As soon as the men came for me,
I was handed over.
I saw how they looked at each-other –
it wasn't what they expected.
My leaving might have been postponed;
you could at least have kissed me.
I couldn't stop my face twisting with tears.
It's the second time I've been a chattel.

I'd slip my guards and run to you,
but they know how to hurt a girl.
I'd be grabbed in darkness,
gifted to one of Priam's sons.

I suppose you gave me because you had to –
yet all these nights without my body and you still don't ask.
Your anger's too slow.
Patroclus, as we parted, whispered:
'Don't cry, it's not for long.'

And besides not claiming me, you even turn down
my return – it's not exactly keen.
I hear Ulysses came to cut a deal,
the plea greased with treasures:
twenty bright hammered-bronze vessels,
twelve thoroughbred horses, and –
though you hardly need them –

lovely Lesbian girls caught fresh from Lesbos.
As a bonus, though you need no wife,
you were offered one of Agamemnon's daughters.

All this you might have paid to buy me back –
yet you refuse me as a gift?
Am I worthless, Achilles?
Has your flimsy love fled so fast?

Does bad luck like to brutalise its victims?
Will it never stop?
I watched your army rape
Lyrnessus, my father's town;
I watched my brothers who shared life
share death;
I watched my husband, laid in bloody dirt,
heave gore up from his chest.

You were my compensation:
my master, brother, husband.
You swore by your mother
that my loss was gain –
but even dowried like this you'd refuse me?
Thrust me back, sneering at riches?

They're even saying that when dawn gleams
you'll unfurl your sails to the cloud-cargoed wind.
When I heard this hideous story,
blood drained from me.

Where are you going? To who?
Where is my comfort?
May I be swallowed by the yawning world,
or ignite by lightning bolt,
before the waters whiten as you row,
before I watch you go.

If you pine for home
I wouldn't slow your fleet.

I'd come as a possession, not a wife.
I'm useful with my hands.
May the most beautiful woman in Achaea
come to your bedroom as a bride:
a bride suited to Jove's royal line!
I, your slave, will spin and the full distaff
grow slender, when I draw the threads.

Only don't let your wife toy with me –
she will resent me.
Don't let her shave my head
while you say, lightly: 'She was mine, once.'
Or let her! Just don't leave me here –
the thought shakes my bones.

Why do you wait? Agamemnon regrets his rage;
Greece lies at your feet.
Can you tame all but your pride?
Why does Hector still harass Greek lines?
Take me to your tent, pick up your armour,
and with Mars' favour overwhelm and awe.
Let me quench the anger I've inspired;
be cause and measure of your wrath.

But no, my words have no currency,
they're nothings.
I know that, master – know I'm no wife
just because I've worked your bed.
A prisoner once called me: 'Mistress' –
I said: 'That name is worse than Slave.'

But by the scant earth over my husband's bones;
by my brothers' souls;
by your head and mine, which touched on the pillow;
by that sword which cost my family;
I swear, Agamemnon never laid a hand on me –
if I lie, cast me away.

If I asked you the same, to swear
you've abstained, you'd refuse.
All Greece thinks you're heartsick
but I know you make music, some tender girl holds you.
Why won't you fight? Because war brings risk,
whilst lyrics, love and dark bring delight.
Safer to clasp a lover,
tinkle on a lyre,
than grab shield and sharp spear
and bear the helmet's pressure.

Yet once renown, not safety, was your aim,
and glory sweet.
Can it be you went to war only to catch me?
When I lost liberty, did you lose heart?
God help us! And may your spear
go quivering to pierce Hector's side.
Greeks, make me ambassadress to Achilles!
I'll mingle kisses with the message
and achieve more than Phoenix, more than Ajax,
with more eloquence than Ulysses!

It would be something though: to hold your neck, to see you,
to stir memories with my breasts.
Though you're savage as your mother's sea
I'd break you with my tears.

May Peleus your father never die,
may Pyrrhus wish for luck like yours,
only recall your Briseis, brave Achilles –
don't torture your poor girl with delays.
Or if you've tired of me,
cause my death as you cause this half-life.
Much more of it will kill;
I lose meat and colour.

If hope leaves too, I'll join my family
and you can say you bid me die.

Why only bid? If your sword penetrates,
does my blood not flow?
Let me be stricken by that sword
from which the gods saved Agamemnon.

But rather protect my life; your gift.
You were my conqueror: I ask you now as friend.
There are more worthwhile objects to destroy,
seek out your enemies.

Whether your ships leave or stay,
as is your right: order me come.

IV: Phaedra to Hippolytus

Phaedra is the wife of Theseus. Her family history is complex – she is a daughter of King Minos of Crete and her mother, Pasiphaë, slept with a bull and gave birth to the Minotaur, her half-brother. Her sister is Ariadne, whom Theseus previously seduced and abandoned before marrying Phaedra.

Now Phaedra has fallen in love with her young stepson, Hippolytus. They are living under the same roof and Theseus is often absent. Her love is unrequited – Hippolytus is very chaste. Robert Graves, in his wonderful, encyclopaedic *The Greek Myths*, suggests that she built the Temple of the Peeping Aphrodite to overlook his gymnasium, where he would run and wrestle stark naked, adding: 'An ancient myrtle-tree stands in the Temple enclosure; Phaedra would jab at its leaves, in frustrated passion, with a jewelled hairpin, and they are still much perforated.' This letter is an attempt at seduction, using every possible argument in an attempt to persuade Hippolytus into an affair.

¶

I wish you well, though lack such wellness, lacking you.

This Cretan maid greets the hero, born of Amazon!

Please read this to the end. How can it harm you?
You might be entertained
by the secrets I spell out.
Even letters from enemies are read!

Three times I've tried to speak to you,
three times my tongue has stopped, sound's failed.
Love should be modest, but though modesty
forbids, it's Love commands me: write.
Love's orders can't be nothing when
it's Love that rules the Gods who rule –
I tried to stop, but Love spoke out:
'Write: his iron heart might yield.'
Well let Love help me then, and heat your marrow
as my marrow, your heart as my heart.

It's not because I'm base I break my marriage vow,
I swear that I was clean till now,
but Love has come, come deep for coming late,
and I am burning, burning in this wounded breast.
As an ox galled by its first yoke,
as a new colt resists its reins,
so does my untried heart rebel
at the submission to restraints, this weight.
If those who learn Love young make it an art,
then love learnt later's fiercer –
you will reap my honour
and we'll be equal in sin.
It's pleasure to pluck fruit from laden branches,
to cull, with just a finger, the new rose –
and if my white life
is to be marked with some rare stain,

I am charred by a worthy flame –
I'd rather Love's forbidden than is mean.
If Juno offered me her Lord and brother, Jove himself,
I think that I would still choose you.

You won't believe it, by the way: I have a new distraction!
I'm stirred to go amongst wild beasts.
Diana's now my goddess, with her bow,
as I cannot help but follow what you follow.
Desire leads me into woods, with nets for deer,
I take my hounds up highest hillsides, let my spear
fly forth, quavering,
or lay down in the grasses,
or delight to drive my carriage through dust;
twist the rein in my steed's mouth.
How I rush like a maenad, god-raving,
like a tambourine-beater at Mount Ida,
or those dryads and horned fauns, those frenzied
by their selves and driven mad –
at least, they tell me so when madness passes.
I stay silent. I know this is Love's torture.

Sometimes I think this Love's a debt I pay.

Perhaps it is my family's fault.
Europa – the beginning of my line –
was loved by Jove, God in bull's form;
my mother, Pasiphaë, raped by
a duped bull, mothered a monster;
a winding thread led Theseus
to slip the labyrinth – my sister helping –
and now I, born of the line of Minos too,
am the latest subjected to these laws.
Isn't it fate that one house conquers us?
Your father caught my sister's heart, you mine:
Theseus and son, you have undone
two sisters – you should both get a prize!

Visiting Eleusis, the city of Ceres,
I wished my land had held me back.
Then you, who'd pleased before, pleased more:
Love pierced my bones deep.
You wore white. Your hair was full of flowers.
Shy, a blush tinged your tanned cheek,
and what others have called hard
in Phaedra's eye was strong.
Away from me with girlish men –
male beauty can't be striven for.
Your hardness suits, your artless fall
of fringe, dirt on your face.
Whether you steer your horse's neck
to make it step tight circles,
or you hurl the lance's shaft
and I gaze on your gallant arm,
or you grasp the hunting spear,
(I'll stop) my eyes Love all of you.

But exhaust your hardness there, outside,
I'm not quarry for your campaign.
What use obeying one goddess
when you snatch dues from Venus?
Nothing endures that goes unrested:
you must repair, renew tired limbs.
Diana knows that if the bow is always bent
it becomes slack, and not a bow.
Cephalus – skilled in killing wildlife –
still yielded to Aurora,
let her sneak from her old husband to his arms.
Often, beneath oak, did Venus
and her Adonis press grass.
Let us too be like them –
a forest without passion is just trees.
I'll come to you, not fearing caves
or boars with slashing tusks.

There is a strip of land two seas attack –
the slender place hears both seas roar –

and I'll live with you there,
Love it more than my home.

Absent Theseus is always absent;
always with his friends. Admit –
his care's for them, not us,
and that's not all that's wrong;
he wounds us both.
He smashed and scattered all my brother's bones;
left my sister in the wild.
Your Amazonian mother lived fiercely like her son,
where is she now? Stabbed by Theseus,
your birth no protection –
yes, and unwed, why?
Would he rather a bastard than an heir?
I bore him sons – each one
he raised an heir to spite you.
Oh I wish that this body, that did you such wrong,
had split –

Why respect your father's bed
that he neglects, degrades?
And if you think me a stepmother who would lie
with her husband's son…just empty names!
Even in Saturn's reign, such virtue
was old-fashioned superstition.
Jove said: "if it feels good,
then how can it be wrong?" Bedded his sister –
bonds of blood hold tightest
when the chain is Venus-forged.

Don't fear the secrecy, it will be easy.
No one will guess. We're family.
They'll compliment our intimacy.
I'll be a fine mother to my son:
the roof that covers will still cover us
and no dour husband's door must be unlocked,
no guard eluded –
as before, our kisses can be open.

You'll be safe with me, even be praised
for lying, blatant, on my couch,
only stop this waiting, hurry –
for you Love will show mercy.
I'm not ashamed to kneel. I beg...

God! Where is my pride, where are my words?
Fallen. I resolved to fight, endure,
but I am overcome,
praying, clutching knees with queenly arms.
Love doesn't care what is befitting,
shame has fled, and all I knew of right.
Forgive me. Please be kind.
Although my father rules the seas
and my ancestors threw lightning
and my grandfather, crowned with rays,
drives around the tepid days,
what does a noble name mean before Love?
If you won't spare me, spare my line.
Jove's island Crete's my Dowry:
take my courtiers for slaves!
Bend, cruel boy! A bull desired
my mother – are you more barbarous still?

By Venus at my side, I pray you spare me,
and that you never love one who will spurn you,
and that the goddess keeps you safe when hunting,
and the dark forest gives you things to kill,
and may Pan and the Satyrs never leave you,
and the boar die, entirely, on your spear,
and may the nymphs you're said to hate – young girls –
slake your awful thirst.

I mix this plea with tears.
You are reading my words. Imagine my tears.

V: Oenone to Paris

Paris is the son of Priam, the king of Troy. When he is born, oracles foretell that the boy will cause the downfall of Troy, and he is given to a shepherd to be left to die on the mountains. The shepherd leaves Paris on the mountainside, but returns days later to find the child has survived and been suckled by a bear, so takes him back to his hut and brings him up. He becomes a strong, handsome young man.

It is when he is living this rural life that he meets Oenone, daughter of a river-god (whose name means 'wine-woman'), and they become lovers.

Afterwards, Paris is restored to his family. Then comes the famous 'Judgement of Paris', where Paris is given a golden apple inscribed 'to the fairest' and told to pick which goddess to give it to – Aphrodite, Hera or Athena (for the Romans Venus, Juno or Minerva). The goddesses attempt to bribe him for the honour. Venus wins by promising him the most beautiful woman in the world – Helen, wife of Menelaus. As this poem begins, Paris has abandoned Oenone for Greece and then returned with the abducted Helen. The oracles' predictions are about to come true.

¶

Will you receive this? Or does your new wife forbid it?
Don't worry – this isn't a Mycenaean hand!
It is the water-nymph, Oenone,
with a complaint to make, if it's allowed.

Who's set their power against my prayers?
What have I done to lose you?
Punishment we deserve is one thing,
but when it's not fair it's depressing.

You were humble when I married you –
I was a daughter of a river-god.
Now you're Priam's son, but – let's talk freely –
then you were a slave I stooped to wed.

Often with your sheep beneath the trees
we'd make a couch of grass and leaves.
Often we sprawled on straw or in low huts,
deep in the hay, to keep from hoar-frost.

Who taught you the chase, the den
where the wild beast kept her cubs?
Often we've stretched the net's wide mesh,
led swift hounds over the hill.

My name is still on beech trees:
OENONE, cut by your knife.
As the trunks swell, so do the letters,
straight and high with my name.

May the poplar by the stream never die,
whose verses, carved in seamy bark
say: *If Paris leaves Oenone and lives,
the waters of Xanthus will run backwards.*

Xanthus, hurry back, reverse to your spring!
Paris left Oenone and exists.
It began one fateful day:
the awful storm of altered love.

Venus, Juno and Minerva (who is fairest in her armour)
came before you naked to be judged.
When you told me of the choice, my heart
was racing; I felt giddy.

Afraid, I took advice, but grandmothers
and old men alike warned: *it's not good.*
Firs were felled, planks hewn, pale green sea
received your polished ships.

We were both upset –
you can't deny you sobbed.
The grapevine grips less
than your arms did my neck.

When you insisted that the wind was wrong
your crew laughed.
You kept coming back for one last kiss
as though your lips couldn't stand 'goodbye.'

But then a breeze rippled slack sails,
and waters fizzed beneath the oars.
I watched your ship disappear;
wet the sand with my tears.

I begged the dolphins for your safety
and by that wish I've lost you.
They've brought you back, but not to me:
with my brutal rival.

A rocky mass looks on the deep,
shoulders the heaving sea.
From there I spied your boat – wanted
to wade through waves.

But then, on the prow, I saw a flash
of frock – it was some Other.
The fresh breeze carried your craft closer;
shivering, I caught a woman's face.

Not only that – why did I stay to see?
She clung to you, cuddled.
I scratched off my make-up;
tore my dress.

Mount Ida echoed with my bawling,
the rocks I love dripped with my tears.
May Helen grieve like this:
may Helen suffer as I suffer!

You pleasure, now, in sluts
who abandon their husbands –
but when you were a shepherd
Oenone was your only one.

I'm not dazzled by jewels or palaces,
or Priam's name (not that Priam
would be shamed by a nymph for a daughter-in-law,
or that Hecuba would hide our kinship.)

But by both worth and desire, I should be princess,
my hands would suit a sceptre.
Don't dismiss me, because we lay on boughs –
I'd be as able in the marriage-bed.

Remember too, this love would never harm you:
would bring no war or vengeance.
Armed men demand your runaway returned –
that's Helen's dowry.

I'd ask whether she should be given back.
Ask Hector, Deiphobus, Polydamas;
take counsel from Antenor and Priam
who are older and cleverer.

It's a bad start, isn't it: to prize a paramour
more than your country? The husband's in the right.
If you're not stupid, don't suppose
one so unfaithful will be true.

Just as Menelaus mourns violated vows,
you'll holler with pain too.
There's no art that makes the penetrated whole;
purity lost is lost.

Is she ardent with lust?
She was for that lonely ass Menelaus too.
Happy Andromache – her man's monogamous!
You should have been more like your brother,

but no – you're lighter than dry leaves
spiralling in shiftless breeze,
lighter than the tips of wheat
parched by many suns.

I remember your sister's prophecy now.
Cassandra sang to me, hair wild; she knew.
'Oenone, you fool! Casting seeds in sand,
ploughing shores with useless oxen.

A Greek cow is coming!
She'll defile your house, your land!
O if only the heifer's unclean ship would sink –
its freight is Trojan blood!'

She ran amok; her slaves wrestled her down.
My yellow hair stood on end.
She is too true a prophetess –
for lo, the cow grazes my pasture.

Beneath her elegance, Helen's just
a slag with a thing for strangers.
They say she was abducted once before,
by, I think – Theseus? Someone like that.

And nothing happened with that young, eager stud?
I'd say so. How do I know? Because *I love*.
Veil her fault and call it rape,
but someone 'stolen' so often's asking for it.

Meanwhile, you're playing around
and I could too, but have been good
– though sexy Satyrs hunt
where I lie hidden in the woods;

though Faunus, pine-needles braiding his horns,
pursued me over Ida's swollen ridge
and Tros, Troy's builder, loved me truly,
ran the secrets of his gifts through my hands.

Whatever herb heals, whatever root
the wide world grows, I now know it –
alas, I can't medicate for heartbreak.
For all my cures I'm uncured.

They say the inventor of these skills
was wounded himself, herding cattle.
The aid I need, no herb or god can give –
but you can help me, you can make me live.

You can, and I deserve it. Pity me!
I bring no bloody Greeks for company.
I'm yours, as I was in our tender youth,
and can be always.

VI: Hypsipyle to Jason

Whilst Jason's betrayal of Medea is widely documented, what is less well-known is that in order to be with Medea he first betrayed Hypsipyle.

Hypsipyle is a compelling character. She is Queen of Lemnos and during her reign Aphrodite cursed the women of the island for neglecting their shrines by giving them extreme body odour. When their husbands found them repellent and took up with female slaves, the women slaughtered all their men. Hypsipyle has shown herself capable of great violence.

But when Jason and the Argonauts wash up on her shores on their quest for the Golden Fleece, she makes herself vulnerable by falling in love with him and becoming pregnant with his twins. Now abandoned for Medea, her cry is one of great rage.

¶

They say your ship's touched Greece,
embellished with a golden fleece.
Please accept my congratulations – though
you might have said yourself.

Perhaps you yearn to return
and winds have kept you from returning,
but there's always messengers.
I deserve a letter instead of rumours –
sacred bulls, crops of men, the sheepskin
snatched from a dragon's den…

To disbelievers, I'd have shown the letter –
proof in your own hand – been proud.
But why complain of neglect?
As long as I'm still yours, I'm indulged.

Gossips say you brought back a foreign witch.
Love is credulous, of course –
so prove this hearsay hasty; groundless.
Recently, a Thessalian visited –
had scarcely stepped upon the step
before I asked: 'How's Jason?'
He stood speechless; eyes stuck to the ground.
I leapt up, panicked –
'Does he live? Must I die too?'
'He lives all right,' he said.
I made him swear, but even then couldn't believe.

When I'd calmed, I asked your story.
He told me of the brazen-footed oxen – how they ploughed;
he told me of the seeding serpent's teeth;
he told me how the earth-grown men sprouted
and fought a civil war, destined to die that very day;
about the sleepless dragon.
'Does he live?' I asked again, muddled
by trust and mistrust.

He was so keen to get the story over with,
I began to realise it would injure me.
Where was the care I'm owed?
Our love wasn't furtive: Juno joined us,
Hymen witnessed it, in his garlanded temple –
yet a foul, blood-soaked Fury
seemed before me, with her luckless torch…

What was the pine-built Argo to me?
What did my land mean to your helmsman?
There was no glittering ram.
At first I meant – though fate prevented it –
for Lemnos' women to drive you out.
We know – too well – how to massacre men;
those sisters are an army for my honour.

Instead I let a man into my city, house and heart.
Two summers fled, two winters thawed.
At the third harvest you set sail,
snivelling such final words:
'We are torn apart, Hypsipyle,
but I am yours as I leave, will return yours.
May the child left heavy in your belly
live and have two parents.'

So you spoke, your fraudulent face slick with tears,
and I remember you could say no more.

You were the last to board the *Argo*.
It flew – the wind fattened its sail,
the sapphire wave slid under keel,
you watched the land, I watched the sea,
ran up the tower to see its breadth,
all wet with tears,
and gazed through tears –
my eyes seemed sharp with love.

For you I made such vows:
they must be paid.

But why fulfil them for Medea to enjoy?
My sick heart surges, blurry
with love and fury. If Jason's mine no more
why slit guts on the altar?
I never felt safe, but my fear was your father –
that he might want an Argive daughter.
I feared Argos, but it was not my nemesis –
my ruin's a barbarian mistress.

It cannot be her looks or personality,
but incantations, spells – she heaves
the unwilling moon from its groove,
disguises the sun's beasts in darkness;
pauses waters, stops streams;
rearranges rocks and woods.

Wild-haired she haunts graveyards, plucks
still-warm skeletons from ash,
sculpts wax poppets, drives
the slender needle through their hearts –
other things I'd rather not know.

Love should be won by merit, not by tricks.
Can you hold such a hag?
Sleep deeply by her side?
She's forced your mouth into a yoke,
hypnotised you like the dragon.
They'll write her name by yours now,
tarnishing your glory,
whilst Pelias' friends impute your deeds to potions,
and such tales are soon believed –
'Not Jason but a girl, Medea,
won the fleece from the ram of Phrixus...'

And can your mother or father like her –
a bride from the frozen north?
Let her find a groom in Scythia's muddy marshes.

Jason, you flap like a fickle breeze –
why are your promises so useless?
You left here mine, and now you're someone else's,
but we can go back to where you left.

You know, too, I've given birth?
Does that make you happy?
It was a precious burden –
Lucina blessed us with twins; a double promise.
They have your likeness
though they've not yet learnt deceit.
I almost sent them to you, as my ambassadors –
but that evil stepmother turned me back.

I fear Medea:
I think no crime beyond her.

She butchered her brother, hurled his flesh on the fields,
why would she hear my pleas?
This is the woman you reject me for –
you're poisoned, fool!
Your bride's a shameless strumpet;
I was chaste.
I rescued my father; she betrayed hers.
Lemnos has my loyalty; she turned on Colchis...

But what's the point, if you simper over sin,
and her crime means she wins?

I don't condone the slaughter here in Lemnos,
but it's no marvel – passion makes women take arms.
Why if, now, unfriendly gales
pushed you to my harbour, with her,
and I came out with twin babies,
surely you'd want the earth to crack?
How would you look at me or look at their faces?
What death would you deserve?
Still, I'd protect you –

I'm merciful –
only dash her brains out, so blood sprayed
my face, your face. For her black arts,
I'd be Medea to Medea.

But if, from his height, Jupiter observes these prayers,
may my usurper
endure my fate herself.
As I'm alone, a new mother with two children –
may she be stripped of babies and a husband.
May she lose these sickening prizes,
and be exiled; a refugee.
A bitter sister and daughter –
she'll be a sour wife and mother.
And when all borders are closed, let her live on air –
wander, a bag-lady, bereft, blood-stained.

Cheated of my marriage, I call down this fate –
may you live on, cursed in your bed.

VII: Dido to Aeneas

In this letter Ovid responds to the fourth book of Virgil's *Aeneid*. Dido is a woman whose previous husband Sychaeus was murdered by her brother. Fleeing, she acquired land in North Africa and used great political guile to establish a city. After the fall of Troy, his city in ruins, Aeneas and his men have landed in this city, Carthage (now in Tunisia), where Dido offers them shelter and hospitality and falls in love with Aeneas. She wants him to stay, but he decides he must travel onwards on his quest to find a new home – it is prophesied that he will found Rome.

This monologue ends with Dido throwing herself onto a pyre – a moment Christopher Marlowe would later render so movingly in his *Tragedy of Dido, Queen of Carthage* with the words: '*sic, sic, juvat ire sub umbras*' ('yes, yes, it pleases me to go into the dark.') In Virgil, Aeneas meets Dido on a later trip to the underworld but she doesn't look at him. T.S. Eliot called this 'the most telling snub' in western literature.

¶

The white swan sings, sinks
into sodden grasses.

I don't hope to move you,
I know the gods oppose these words.
But I've lost reason, reputation, a clean body –
words are a small loss.

Are you sure you want to go?
To leave pitiful Dido?
Are you set, Aeneas, on unfettering moorings, promises,
for made-up kingdoms, Italy, who-knows-where?

Are you not touched by new Carthage, her soaring walls,
her offer to give you power?
Turn away from the past. You've found this place –
why seek another, forever, through the whole wide world?

And this land of desire, who will give it you?
Who gives their fields to a stranger?
Will there be a second love, a second Dido,
more pledges and faking?
When will chance grant you a city like this –
let you watch your people from a high castle?
And even if gods grant every whim, with no delay –
who will love you like I do?

I am an inferno. Love burns like sulphur,
wax, incense. This is incineration.
Every wakeful minute, my eyes weld to Aeneas;
he quickens me, day and night.
He's ungrateful, ignores my generosity.
I should be glad he goes,
but however ill he thinks of me, can't hate –
I call him cheat, but love him so.

Venus, spare your daughter-in-law –
Aeneas must fight for your camp.
I let all my love go to him, let him
let me look after him!

But I invent fictions.
His heart is not his mother's heart.
Aeneas, you must have been born
with resin for blood or a stone in your chest,
or out of the sea you plan to take to,
despite all threats.

Why go? Rains rise to stay you.
The North wind tips the rolling waters.
What I wanted from you, storms give instead –
the roar and surge more just.
But I'm not brave enough, in my misjudgement,
to have you perish in the sea.
It is expensive, your hatred, if quitting me
you think it's cheap to die.

Still, soon it will calm, shells settle.
If only you were so mutable –
but if you're mortal, surely you must be.
What here's worse than seething seas?
Why trust foam that thrashed you?
Even untying ropes when water's sleek,
you'll find how many tears make up the deep.

And breaking faith tempts the breakers.
They say the place punishes
above all for wronged love, as Venus rose
unclothed from brine.
I fear undoing my undoer – harming he who harms –
my enemy shipwrecked; gulping on sea.
I pray you live to be undone, to see
the thing you've done.

Imagine a squall sweeps you up (may it not)
what will flood your last thoughts?
Remembered falsehood?
My suicidal self?
Will your abandoned bride float before you:
sorrow-weighted, hair streaming, blood-blotched?
You'll have to plead for mercy
from thrown thunderbolts.

So wait – let the seas and cruelty subside;
a safe voyage will reward your patience.
Let your son Iulus be saved at least,
as it's enough to cause my death,
and like your household gods, he's done nothing wrong –
were they only snatched from flames to smash in surf?
Yet perhaps you never carried your relics
and they're just an excuse
for a dissembler
and I'm not your first victim.

Where's your son's mother? In your apathy,
you left her behind and she died.
Did you tell me this story as a warning?

Burn me: I'm defective, I deserve it.

And you, too, are condemned by the gods –
seven years you've been buffeted.
A castaway when I helped you,
offering a kingdom when I scarcely knew your name –
I wish that had been all
and our story never told.

That ghastly day was my ruin: the sudden drench
of rain from blue-black heavens drove us into a cavern.
I heard voices – I thought it nymphs,
but the Furies were uttering my fate.

Sullied purity, punish me –
I owe it to Sychaeus, my first husband.
Overcome with shame, I went to his shrine,
his marble statue under green branches.
Four times it echoed with a voice I knew.
Tenderly, he said: 'Come.'

I come, Sychaeus, your wife is coming
and is sorry she has been so slow!
Forgive me. My ravisher was skilled
and sucked the horror from the sin.
Loyalty to his father and divine mother
gave me hope that he'd be true –
if I lapsed, it wasn't for bad reasons;
if he stays, I have no regrets.

So my life pursues the same predictable pattern
and will now, to the end.
My husband crumpled in blood before the altar;
my gruesome brother took the pickings.
Exiled, I had to leave the ashes,
flee enemies down grim paths.

Evading my brother, I bought this coast
I have offered you, traitor –
established a city, founded wide-spanning walls
that neighbours envied.
Foreign and a woman, I was attacked;
had hardly ordered makeshift gates, but they needed defence.
A thousand suitors wooed, then whined
that I preferred outsiders.

Why don't you tie me up and give me to them?
I'd submit.
Or how about my brother, whose hand could be sprinkled
with my blood, as it is my husband's blood?
Lay down your relics: your fingers profane them.
Unholy hands mustn't pray.

When you worship the gods who escaped from fire,
they grieve that they escaped from fire.

I could be pregnant too –
a part of you stashed in my flesh.
Some poor baby might suffer my destiny
and you'll murder your unborn child.
Your son's brother will die with his mother:
entangled, both must pay.

'But God forces us to go.' Would he'd forced you not to come –
Trojan feet never pressed our earth!
Is this, by any chance, the god who guided you
to spend long years, bruised by waters?
A reborn Troy couldn't be worth that
if it thrived as it did in Hector's day.
You seek not the Simois, but the swelling Tiber,
yet when you reach it you'll be a stranger.
The land you quest for cloaks itself;
shuns your keel.
When you get there you'll be old.

End this drifting! Choose me,
choose my dowry, people, wealth.
Remake Troy in Carthage –
you'll be happy here as king.
If you're zealous for war, if Iulus needs
a field to prove prowess and earn glory,
I can find enemies.
You won't lack anything: peace or conflict.
But by your mother, your brother, his arrows,
by all your divine patrons,
may you save your race,
may that inhuman war be your last loss...

I beg you, spare this house, its unconditional gift –
what am I charged with, but love?
I am not from Phthia or Mycenae,
you've not been wronged by my relatives.

If you're ashamed to call me wife, call me mistress:
to be yours, I'll be anything.

I know the spume that breaks on Africa's beaches,
what it allows and denies.
When it permits, you'll give your canvas to the wind
but now slippery seaweed snags your ship.
Trust me to watch the weather, you'll go later –
even if you wanted it, I wouldn't let you stay!
Your crew needs sleep, your fleet care,
a pause is needed for repair.
I ask for time.
Let my love and sea grow milder,
let me learn how to endure.

Relent or I'll pour my life out:
your cruelty can't last.
If only you could see me writing
with the sword you gave me on my knee,
tears sliding across cheeks, dripping to the drawn blade
which will soon be wet with blood.
Thanks to your gift,
my death won't cost me much.

This isn't the first time I'll feel a weapon's thrust –
I've been run through by mad love.

Anna, oh my sister, poor witness –
you'll soon give my ash a last grace.
When the pyre's fire's consumed me,
don't carve 'wife of Sychaeus', carve:
'Aeneas gave cause and sword,
but Dido destroyed herself.'

VIII: Hermione to Orestes

Hermione is the daughter of Mycenaean king Menelaus and his wife Helen. During the Trojan War (fought over her mother), in her parents' absence, Hermione's grandfather promises her to Orestes, whom she falls in love with. However, her father then insists Hermione marry Pyrrhus, Achilles' son, as the Greeks need to pacify Achilles. Hermione is deeply unhappy with this new match. Although this version of the story scarcely refers to it, in many tellings the problem is compounded by Pyrrhus' concubine Andromache.

Orestes himself has a complicated family background – the son of Agamemnon, he has just killed his mother, Clytemnestra, and her lover Aegisthus, in order to avenge his father's murder (the subject of Aeschylus's great cycle of tragedies *The Oresteia*). Hermione seems to take this as evidence of his courage, hoping it will make him willing to fight for her.

¶

Pyrrhus is stubborn like his father –
mocks every natural law to keep me here.
I don't consent in bed
but my girlish hands can't keep him off.

I scream: 'what have you done?'
I say I have a master already.
He's deaf as water when I cry your name, Orestes –
drags and dishevels me.

It wouldn't be any worse if Sparta had been taken,
and I was a barbarian slave.
Andromache wasn't abused so badly
when fire destroyed Troy.

If you care, Orestes,
you must claim what's yours.
You'd retaliate for opened gates; a stolen herd.
Why so slow when it's your wife?

Copy my father: had he sulked, spineless,
in empty halls, Helen would still be with Paris.
Yet don't build a thousand ships with bulging sails,
don't arm battalions – come yourself.

It's not unseemly to seek me
or fight fiercely for the love of our bed.
We have the same grandfather –
if you weren't my husband, we'd be cousins.

Husband, help your wife; brother, your sister!
Both bonds bind you to duty.
My grandfather Tyndareus,
wise and experienced, gave me to you.

Ignorant of this, with no right,
my father promised me to Achilles' son.
When I wed you, it hurt no one;
marrying Pyrrhus hurts you.

My father'll forgive our love, I'm sure –
he's fallen to Love's darts before.
He has to concede what he's allowed himself –
my mother set the precedent.

You are to me as father was to mother,
and Pyrrhus is the Trojan.
Let him gloat about his father's deeds!
You can brag about your father too:

Agamemnon, son of Tantalus, ruled even Achilles –
just a soldier to that king of kings.
You, too, have ancestors – Pelops and his father.
If you count, you're just five places from Jove!

And you're not without prowess – it was a bleak task,
but what could you do? Your father forced it.
You should be famed for more glorious deeds,
but your cause was fixed, not chosen.

You did your duty: Aegisthus' blood
splattered the red stains of your father's –
but Pyrrhus smears you with blame,
and when I glare, doesn't even flinch.

I'm breaking with anger, my face flares up;
I'm pounding with pent-up pain.
To insult you in my presence,
when I've no power to strike!

I can sob, at least.
Salt-water streams in rivers to my breast.
It's all I have, this gush;
my cheeks bloat, ugly with tears.

Is the family curse still with us –
that all women must be raped?
I shan't go on about that cheating swan;
Jove squatting in pale plumage.

Or how Hippodamia, where sea's sundered,
was kidnapped by a stranger.
How Helen was stolen across seas
by that man from Mount Ida,

a man welcomed as a guest,
and how all Greece rose to bring her back.
I barely recall that time, yet do –
everything was grief.

My grandfather wept, Phoebe, the twins;
Leda prayed to gods and Jove.
As for me, chewing my downy hair, I cried:
'Mummy, don't leave me behind!'

My father left too. Whilst he was gone
I was passed to you, to secure the line.
If only Achilles had escaped Apollo's bow!
He would condemn his son.

It wasn't his pleasure, and wouldn't be now
to see a husband weep for a lost wife.
What have I done that Heaven's set against me?
To which sick star should I complain?

As a child I had no mother, father fought –
they weren't dead, but I was an orphan.
You weren't there, mother,
for the first, stammered words of your small girl.

I couldn't put my teeny arms around your neck,
or be a weight on your lap.
You didn't care.
When I wed, no mother helped me prepare.

And then when you came back, I ran to meet you
and I didn't even know your face,
and then I realised you were Helen, the most beautiful,
and you asked which one I was.

My only luck was in this marriage
which I'll lose if he won't fight.
If my father won the war
why am I am Pyrrhus' captive?

I find succour when the sun
urges his horses scale the sky,
but night drags me, squirming,
to the bed

and I lie, welling up, on those grimy sheets;
wince when my enemy approaches.
Often, in panic, I writhe –
accidentally touch

his body, reel with horror,
my skin soiled.
Often, in sleep, I say your name, Orestes:
is that a good sign?

By our cursed family; by that parent
who rattles earth and sea;
by your father's bones – my uncle's –
that, thanks to you, rest easy:

I swear now, I shall be a young corpse
or else – descendant of Tantalus – yours.

IX: Deianira to Hercules

Hercules, illegitimate son of Jove and 'demi-God', has won Deianira twice. First he fought the river-god Achelous for her hand in marriage. After this, a centaur called Nessus attempted to rape Deianira whilst ferrying her across a river – Hercules killed him with an arrow tipped with the Hydra's venom. As he lay dying, Nessus told Deianira to take some of his blood, as it would be a powerful love potion (not mentioning its toxicity).

Now, as wife of Hercules, Deianira is stuck at home, constantly hearing reports and rumours of his escapades. The goddess Juno, who hates him for his status as Jove's half-son, is stirring up trouble. With his twelve famous labours Hercules has brought Deianira glory, but his adventures with women also bring humiliation. He was recently enslaved by Omphale, Queen of Lydia (now western Anatolia in Turkey) and there are rumours that this inversion of gender roles involved him dressing up in women's' clothes. He has also just defeated Oechalia with his army, bringing home the king's lovely daughter Iole as a prize of war. Deianira wants him to stop displaying his affairs so openly and love only her.

¶

I'm glad you've beaten Oechalia,
but hear the winner is the loser;
vicious rumours undermine your exploits.
Twelve labours couldn't break you,
but they say Iole has you tamed.

Your stepmother Juno will be thrilled
to hear you've spoilt your reputation,
but not great Jove who, some say, found
one night too short for your conception.

Venus harms you more than Juno:
Juno spurred glory, but Venus has her foot on your throat.

Look at the circle of earth you've made peaceful,
wherever azure waters wrap the land.
You've brought security to seas
from sunset-west to sunrise-east.
You once held heaven on your back,
took the strain of stars from Atlas.
What was the use, if your celebrity
only spreads word of your scandals?

Are you the baby who choked two snakes in the cot?
You were worthy of Jove then,
but did you lose it,
your promise dwindling with age?
You overcame so many obstacles,
but lust overcomes you.

I'm envied for the match I made –
daughter-in-law to thunderous Jove –
but as your partner I'm an ill-matched steer,
hitched badly to the plough.
It's no honour – it's hard work.
A happy marriage should be one between equals,

but you're always gone – more guest than husband –
chasing some myth or monster.
I'm lonely, desperate, bored.
Images torture me:
serpents, boars and lions,
three-throated, hungering hounds.

Prophecies in entrails, day dreams, omens –
they all stir my stress.
I catch at murmurs, common chit-chat.
Fear's lost in hope, then hope to fear.

Your mother's gone: the god's love cost her dearly.
Your father and son aren't here.
It's me who has to cope with Juno's festering rage.

Isn't this enough?
Must you add your affairs, your sown oats?
The rape in the woods; that gang of sisters you deflowered;
and the new low of knocking up Lydia's queen.

And trickles of gossip soon muttered
of necklaces round your thick neck!
Are you shameless,
braceletting your brawn with gold and jewels?
To think: your muscles squeezed the lion
whose pelt you wear,
yet you wove women's' ribbons through your hair!
And modelling the Lydian belt,
like Miss Playful. You're sick – *sick*.

Didn't you think of savage Diomedes,
feeding horses human flesh?
Had banished Busiris seen you dressed like that
he'd have blushed.
Antaeus would have torn out your ribbons –
mortified at your unmanliness.
They say she *frightened* you.
They say you held wool-baskets like a girl.

Didn't your legendary hand
flinch from working wool?
How often, when you twisted threads, your big hands
must have broken the spindle...

At her feet,
did you tell tales best forgotten in that state –
of serpents throttled, coiling
their length around your tiny child's-fingers;
the boar's lair amongst the cypress-trees,
his size jolting the earth?

Did you forget the skulls nailed up in Thracian homes,
or the mares plump with slain men?
Did you forget the triple-headed Geryon,
rich with cattle?
The dog Cerberus, one-bodied but three-jawed,
his hair tangled with snake,
or the Hydra, fertile with her hurt,
who sprang back, plural, from each wound?
Did you mention your left arm pinning the mass
as you strangled the giant?
The horsey, hybrid centaurs you wiped out
on the Thessalian hills?

Could you tell anecdotes in a fashionable gown?
Did cross-dressing not affect your voice?

The Queen even dragged up in your armour –
humiliating the hero.
Go on, puff yourself up, brag of your bravery,
but she was the man.
You're less than her, who mastered the so-called master.
Shame, that your shaggy lion-skin
showed-off a woman's cleavage!
She wore your spoils, not lion's spoils –
you beat the beast, but she beat you.
She gripped your venom-tipped darts,
who'd scarcely held wool's weight before;

hefted your monster-mashing club;
posed admiringly in mirrors!

Such talk, though, comes with fame.
It pained my ears, but I could doubt it.
But now I'm forced to see Iole – the foreign concubine –
I'm gutted.

I can't turn away; I'm forced to watch
that captive paraded through the city.
Yet she doesn't come like captives –
all bad hair and gloomy faces –
but struts, glamorous in gold
such as you wore in Phrygia.
She's proud before the crowds, head up,
as if she's won and her father still lives.

Perhaps you'll dump me, Deianira,
and my rival climb from mistress to wife.
You'll join Iole and yourself
together in a shameful, sham marriage.
I can't even think about it – I get the shivers;
my numb hands slump in my lap...

I was once one of your many conquests too,
but you made me respectable;
fought twice for your wife –

fought the river-god Achelous
until he bawled, picked up his horns, soaked
his mashed forehead in the murk;

fought the ferryman Nessus when he tried to rape me,
made him sink beneath lotus blooms,
blood pumping into water...

But why do I go on? As I write, news arrives.

There's reports that you're dying
from a poisoned shirt I gave you. But...

No. No –
what have I done in my madness?

They'll cry: 'Bitch! Why not kill yourself?
Will our hero be torn to death on Oeta's height
whilst you live on, a black widow?
If you've ever deserved the name wife,
suicide will show togetherness!'

Hercules Horror: Wicked Wife Still Lives

They'll dig into my family's tragic story:
Agrius on the throne, whilst Oeneus dribbles with age,
the exiled brother, the other's death by fire,
how my mother stabbed herself in the heart...

Deianira, you bitch – why not kill yourself?
Why wait for lies
about how I planned his murder?
It was Nessus – arrow stuck from his spurting chest,
he dipped that shirt in his blood.
Lied: 'This has power over love'.
I was tricked; it was toxic.

Poison Shirt Shock: Demands for Deianira's Death

All right then –
goodbye father, sister, brother,
nation, the bright lights, husband (could you but live)
and, finally, my son: goodbye.

X: Ariadne to Theseus

Ariadne's story begins with her father, King Minos of Crete, attacking Athens when it is weakened by disease and its inhabitants cannot defend themselves. They make a truce, with the condition that every nine years Athens sends seven boys and seven girls to feed the Minotaur, the monstrous outcome of Minos' wife Pasiphaë falling in love with a white bull (she persuaded the inventor Daedalus to make her a cowhide frame to hide in so the bull could mount her).

One year Theseus, son of the Athenian king Aegeus, volunteers to join the group, hoping to kill the Minotaur. He attracts the attention of Ariadne, who helps him by giving him a ball of string so he can find his way through the labyrinth. Theseus kills the Minotaur then leaves Crete, taking Ariadne with him as she has betrayed her father and brother. But he abandons her on the barren island of Dia, now known as Naxos.

¶

Untamed beasts are more tender than you;
they could not be less trustworthy.
I write this letter from the beach, Theseus,
where your ship sailed off without me;
the shore on which my sleep and you
have left me so brutally betrayed.

At that time when the island is first frost-spangled
and hidden birds first lament,
half-waking, listless, I turned
with fumbling hands to hold you –
you were not there. I drew back, tried again,
my arms groped the whole bed – you weren't there.
Fear slapped me awake: I lurched up,
tumbled headlong from the empty bed.
My hands searched my breasts; the hair
that was mazy with sleep.

The moon shone. I looked at the shore,
and could see nothing but shore,
and began to run – this way, that – confused,
the loose sand pulling at my feet,
all the while crying: 'Theseus!' along the long beach,
as the hollow stones gave me back your name
every time I called for you; the whole island called for you,
moved to help me in my grief.

A mountain exists, scraps of green at the top;
it juts, eaten away by hoarse water.
I climbed it, somehow, and from the peak
scanned the whole deep sea.
There – thrashed by fierce winds –
I saw your sails full of gale
and as I saw, or thought I saw, this unfair sight
I turned dull as ice.
But no – anguish spurned rest, it roused;

goaded me to scream with all my strength:
'Cruel Theseus, where are you racing? Come back!
Turn round your ship- she hasn't all her crew!'

So I cried, and when my voice failed I hit myself;
the blows bled into my words.
I thought you'd see, if you couldn't hear;
I was signalling you with my hands.
On a tree-branch I tied my flickering veil
to remind you of who you'd forgotten –

until at last you were swept beyond my vision.
Only then did I cry:
my eyes had been sluggish with shock.
But what else to do, now they couldn't see your sails?

Alone, loose hair flying, I have wandered
like a Bacchant in her ecstasy,
or sat on chilly pebbles to watch the sea,
as much a stone as stone.
Over and over, I've looked at our bed,
but it won't show us together.
I touch the imprint you left – all that's left –
and the covers that grew warm beneath your legs.
I lie down, face-down; damp the bed with beading tears.
'Two of us pressed you – give him back!
We came to you together – how did we rise apart?
Faithless bed – where is he?'

What am I to do? I am alone, the island wild.
There are no human traces; no cattle;
it is encircled by a sea with no sailors;
no ships follow these dubious paths.
And suppose I found people, and wind, and a ship –
where to go? My father's land's forbidden.
Even if a lucky craft slid on smooth seas,
Aeolus tempering winds, I'd be an exile.
O Crete, with your hundred cities –
I cannot look at you.

No, I betrayed my father
and my father's land (dear words)
when after your victory, to keep you from death
in the winding dark, I gave you a thread.
You said: 'By these dangers I swear you'll be mine,
so long as we both shall live.'

We both live, Theseus, but I'm not yours –
or I think I live, at least, though I feel buried.
You should have slain me with the blow that brained my brother;
oaths dissolve with death.
Now not only my own pain, but all the pain
of all the women left behind consumes my mind
and a thousand ways of dying hound my mind
and death seems better than delay.

Each moment – here, there – I look for wolves
to open up my guts with teeth.
Does this shore breed tawny lions?
Shelter tigers? Deep waters
have been known to slop up massive seals – and what stops
the plunge of men's swords into my lungs?

I'm indifferent. My only fear is slavery
and those who'd make me spin with shackled hands –
I, whose father was Minos,
who (I recall vividly) was your fiancé.

I look on sea and land and the broad shore
and there are enemies everywhere.
The sky is there, but I fear gods!
I'm helpless, meat for maws of famished beasts;
and if men are here, I don't trust them:
you've taught suspicion of strangers.

If only Androgeos was alive; if only Athens
had not paid its debt with doomed children.
If only you hadn't clubbed to mush
that part-bull, part-man;

I hadn't slipped the thread that led
a path, caught and passed through hands.
It is no wonder you won,
the monster's length thumping Cretan soil,
his horns could not gash your heart –
your naked chest was safe.
In there is flint;
you are harsher than rocks.

And then this, here: how slumber pinned me, inert –
better to be weighted; sink to never-ending night.
And the mean winds too, all over-keen;
breeze racing to rise my tears.
How hateful that the hand that kills me killed my brother;
how vile the vow – that empty word – you gave.
It was a conspiracy: sleep and wind and word –
three traitors to one girl!

Am I to die then, and not see my mother cry?
Shall no one finger shut my eyes?
Must my soul journey through alien air,
with no arrangement of limbs; no anointment?
Will hovering birds peck my unburied bones?
Is this the burial I'm owed?

You will go home,
but when you stand tall amongst your thronging fans,
telling of the Minotaur's death,
of those twisting halls cut from stone,
tell them too, of me, abandoned here alone –
don't neglect me, amongst your boasts!

Aegeus is not your father, Aethra not your mother –
you must have been born to boulders and depths.

I pray you saw me from your high stern;
that my sad shape hurt your heart.
Yet look upon me now – picture me in your mind –
clinging to a crag, whipped by wandering waves.

See my hair, mussed up like a mourner's,
my dress heavy with tears as if with rain.
I am a blasted crop.
My handwriting falters.

Though you do not deserve it, don't worry –
I ask nothing in return for all I did.
But stop this torture – if I hadn't saved you,
I still wouldn't deserve this.
My hands are tired of bashing my breast,
see them stretch towards you over the vast sea –
look at my torn hair!
By the tears you are moving down my face,
turn your ship, your sail, ride back to me.

If I've died already, I'd still want you to carry my bones.

XI: Canace to Macareus

Canace is writing to her brother, Macareus, who is also her lover and the father of her child. But there is no blame here or suggestion of abuse – it is her father whom she rails against: Aeolus, who will not forgive them for their incestuous relationship. Aeolus was the name of both the God of the winds and the Thessalian king who fathered Canace and Macareus – here Ovid seems to have blended the two figures.

¶

If what I write is blotted or obscure,
the book is probably blood-stained.
My right hand holds a pen, the other a blade,
the paper is unrolled on my lap.

I am Aeolus' daughter, writing to my brother.
This image, at least, might please our father.
I wish he were here to watch me die –
he should see the death he orders,
though, harsher than his own east-winds,
he'd look dry-eyed at my wounds.

He's just like his savage gusts –
his tempests suit his temper.
Notus, Zephyr, Aquilo, Eurus,
he rules them all
but not his blustering wrath;
beside his flaws, his kingdom looks tiny.

What does it matter that my grandfathers' names touch the skies?
That Jove is my kin?
Is the blade less deadly?

It feels weird in my woman's hand.

Macareus, I wish we had not slept together
until after I had died.
Why, brother, did you love me more than a brother?
Why have I been what a sister shouldn't be?

I was illuminated by love
and felt some god was glowing in my heart.
I turned ash, wasted all my flesh.
My unwilling mouth could scarcely eat.
Uneasy sleep made every night a year
that was not pain, yet made me moan.

I couldn't yet think why, not knowing love,
but love it was.

The first to diagnose my trouble was my nurse.
She said: 'you're in love!'
I flushed, and shame bent my eyes to my chest;
wordlessly I confessed.

And soon our incest fattened, inside,
my weak frame struggled with its secret.
Her bold hands spooned me every herb or medicine,
tried every trick to drive it out.
It was all I ever kept from you –
that growing burden –
but it was too full of life, the little thing,
withstood all arts and enemies.

Nine times the fairest moon rose. The tenth time
the moon impelled her pale horses
I shuddered with sharp pangs.
I was a soldier new to battle.
I screamed, but the nurse said: 'Why advertise your fault?'
She stopped my crying lips.
What could I do? It was agony
but her and fear and guilt told me: shut up.
I bit my lip, swallowed words,
drank tears from my own eyes.

I could see Death. Lucina wouldn't help.
And Death, if I died, would show my shame.
But then you were leaning over,
pushing my hair from my face, holding me,
saying: 'Sister, sister, my beloved,
if you die I'll die too.
Please hope. I want to marry you.
You have my child, should be my wife.'
I was dead, yet you resuscitated me,
our baby was born from my womb.

But why be glad? Our father sat in his hall,
and we had to hide the truth.
Carefully, my nurse concealed the child
with grapes and olive branches,
made mock prayers and sacrifices
so neighbours and my father let her pass.
She'd crossed the room, was near the threshold –
then that treacherous wail.
He seized it. Saw the fraud,
his maddened howl broke the palace walls.

As the ocean judders in light breeze,
as warm winds shake the ash-tree,
my limbs trembled;
my bed seemed to quake in sympathy.
He whirled in, yelling filth,
scarcely kept himself from hitting my face.
I was mute with it all, I wept
but my tongue was stunned with fear.

His decree: his grandson should be exposed.
Teeth and beaks would clean his bones.
Our baby cried. He knew what was meant.
He was pleading.

Brother, you must know from your own mind
what I felt when our flesh
was taken into the deep forest
to be harrowed by wolves.
Only when our father left my bedroom
did I try to hurt myself.

Then one of his guards entered
and said, as though sorry:
'Aeolus sends this blade to you' – he handed me it –
'He says you know what you deserve.'

I do know. I'm brave enough.
I shall bury my father's gift in my chest.

What a father, to bring such presents to a marriage!
Do such dowries make a daughter rich?
Leave, god of weddings, with your torches –
fly in fear from these sick halls.
Black Furies, I'll have fires
for my cremation instead.

I hope our sisters' weddings may be happier,
that they recall me, lost.
My newborn – did he sin in so few hours?
Who did he harm?
If he deserved it, judge him, but –
poor mite, he suffers for his mother.

O my boy, my grief, prey of ravening beasts,
born to be torn into pieces.
Sad pledge of my unhallowed love,
this was your first and last day.
I cannot keen or shave my hair,
I cannot lean over you
or cull a kiss from your cold lips.

Vicious animals are ripping him apart –
I must follow my child's shade; deal the stroke.
I won't be called a mother or bereaved for long!
You, for whom your sister always hoped,
I entreat to find his scattered bones
so he can share his mother's tomb;
one small urn hold us both.

Live. Remember. Pour tears on the wound.
Don't ever shrink from me or our love.

Fulfil the wish of a sister you loved too well,
as I fulfil our father's wish.

XII: Medea to Jason

Medea is a figure who fascinated Ovid – she also figures in the *Metamorphoses* and he wrote a tragedy about her which has been lost.

She is a daughter of the King of Colchis (now Georgia), a barbarian and priestess of the underworld goddess Hecate, adept at witchcraft, who helps Jason on his quest for the Golden Fleece. This aid includes helping him to kill her brother, Absyrtus, dismembering his body and throwing the parts from their ship as they leave Colchis, so those in pursuit have to collect the limbs whilst they get away.

They have ended up in Corinth in Greece, where they have two sons. But the Corinthians do not like the sorceress, and when Jason is offered the hand of King Creon's daughter Creusa, a Greek, he accepts and decides to banish Medea. This is a decision that will lead to tragic consequences most famously dramatised by Euripides.

¶

And yet for you, I recall, I – the Queen of Colchis –
could find time when you asked me for help.

That was when three sisters who spin out fates
should have unwound my thread.
Better to die then.
Everything since has been punishment.

Why did that ship made from Pelion's wood,
rowed by young arms, seek the golden fleece?
Why did we cast eye upon the *Argo*?
Why did your crew sup the waters of the Phasis?
Why did I delight in your blondeness, your charm,
the false grace of your tongue?

Yet I did delight, too much, or when your ship was beached
to unload your heroes, your self,
you'd have met bulls with burning breath
without anointment by my spells;
would have scattered such seeds
you would have planted death.
How much treason, you scum, would have died with you.
I would not suffer as I do.

There is pleasure in reproaching the ungrateful
with favours done. It is my only fun.
In your untried craft you came
and landed on our rich shore,
where I was what your new bride is today:
her father's wealthy, so was mine.

He entertained your Greek youths,
you lolled your limbs on his embroidered couch.
It was then that I saw you, began to know you,
began my downfall. I saw you
and was undone – not with ordinary fire,

but the fire of pine-torches lit for worship.
And you were handsome, true, but fate
dragged me down too; your eyes blinded my eyes.
You knew it, traitor, didn't you? Love can't hide:
its flame betrays itself.

Meanwhile, you had to force three bulls
to bow and pull the plough –
and not just horned,
but Mars' bulls, blaze-breathed,
their hooves hard bronze, their nostrils
blasted black with soot.
Besides this, you'd to scatter
seeds that started men who'd spring
up, bones born of soil, with swords to slay you;
a dark harvest for its sower.
Eluding the eyes of the guard that never sleeps
was your last task.

Aeëtes' speech finished. Everyone stood, sadly,
removed the table, the violet-draped couch.
How far away your thoughts were then
from Creusa or her dowry or her proud father.
You left in fear and as you went
my eyes were wet, my mouth could scarcely shape 'goodbye'.

I lay in my bedroom.
All night I hurt and cried.
I saw the beasts, the dreadful crop,
the snake's unblinking eyes:
I felt both fear and love, and fear increases love.

At dawn my dearest sister found me
face down in despair with loosened hair,
tears everywhere.
She asked aid for your Argonauts:
she prayed and I implored and you were saved.

There is a grove, mournful with pines and oak,
sun cannot enter.
There is in it – or was – a shrine;
Diana made of gold by rough hands.
Do you know the place? Or does it slip your mind along with me?
We met there and your faithless lips said:
'My fortune lies in your hands.
My life or death lies in your hands.
To have the power to ruin is enough, if power is pleasure,
but saving me will bring you greater glory.
O maiden, pity me, pity my men,
be kind and mine.
If it isn't beneath you to wed me –
though how can I hope it? –
may my soul disappear
before another bride comes to my bed.'

Words like these – and more – and your hand clutching my hand
moved my naive heart.
I even saw tears – or were they part of your lie?
How fast, child that I was, your words ensnared me.
You collared the bulls with unsinged hand,
your plough cleaved land,
you sowed the poisoned teeth as seed
and warriors burst up with sword and shield
and despite my potions
I sat pale with terror as they grew,
until – the miracle – those newborn brothers drew
arms to fight themselves.

And look: rattling its scales, the unsleeping
beast sweeps floor with twisting belly.
Where was your rich dowry then?
Where was your royal bride of Ephyre?
It was I – the woman now barbarian to you,
poor and hateful – who closed the lids
of scorching eyes with drugs that brought on sleep,
and gave you your beloved fleece.
I fleeced my father; left my throne, my home.

My prize was exile. Thief –
you took my innocence!

I miss my mother and my sisters.
But my brother – I didn't leave him behind.
I can't write it –

My hand's strong enough to do it, but not write it!

I should have been torn limb from limb too, with him,
and yet, beyond fear, I never feared
trusting myself and my guilt to the sea.
Where is justice? Where are the gods?
We should have been drowned for our treachery and trust.
I wish the clashing rocks had caught and crushed our bones
so mine were mashed with yours;
that Scylla's dogs had gorged on us –
it's fit she kills ungrateful men –
that she that sucks and spews
had brought us, too, beneath Sicilian waves.

But no: safe, victorious, you returned to your town,
laid the fleece down before your gods.

And Pelias' daughters... Must I tell again
how they hacked their father into pieces?
Others blamed me, but you mustn't –
my crime was that I tricked those girls for you.
Yet you dared – words fail my fury –
you dared to say: 'Leave our palace.'

At your bidding I left with our two children
and that stalker, love,
when suddenly we heard the wedding chant
and my eyes saw glinting torches,
and pipes poured notes, for you a wedding song,
for me more painful than a funeral dirge.
Things tilted. I couldn't yet believe such wickedness,
but still, my chest grew chill.

The crowd pressed on, cried: 'Hymen, O Hymenaeus!'
the cry more dreadful the nearer it got.
My slaves wept, but tried to hide their tears –
who'd break such ill news?
And it's true, better I hadn't known,
but my heart was heavy, as if I knew,
and when our youngest child, keen to see,
stood at the door's outer threshold,
cried: 'Mother! Come out! There's a procession!
Daddy leads it in bright gold, driving the horses!'
I slashed my cloak, I beat myself,
I scraped my face with merciless nails.
I could not help but storm the mob and rip
garlands from pretty hair, I scarce
could keep from screaming, hair all torn:
'He's mine' and holding you.

Be happy, my poor father; my country!
Ghost of my brother, here's your payment.
I've lost my title, land and home,
my husband, who for me was all of them.
It seems I can tame serpents
but not a man.
I held back fire with my enchantments
but cannot stand the melt of my own lust.

My incantations, herbs and art have abandoned me,
no one will help; potent Hecate does nothing.
I take no happiness in day; nights are bitter vigils.
Gentle sleep's gone too.
I charmed dragons to doze, but can't do this for myself:
I can aid others, not myself.
The limbs I saved entwine around a whore's;
she eats the fruit.

Perhaps, when you show off for your silly wife,
you will insult my foreign ways and face
to please her:
well, let her mock!

Let her laugh on her high, purple bed.
Soon she'll scream and blister far worse than me.
Whilst sword, fire and poison are near my hand
no enemy of mine will go unpunished.

But if you can still be touched by pleas, hear these words –
words too meek for my proud self:
I am a supplicant to you, as you have been to me,
I cast myself at your feet.
If I seem cheap, at least be kind to our children.
She'll be a hard stepmother.
They look like you, too much:
when I see them tears drop from my eyes.
I beg by the gods, my grandfather the sun,
our sons and all I've done,
restore me to the bed for which I lost everything.
Help me as I helped you.
I don't ask you to fight
bulls, men or snakes:
it is you I ask for, you I've earned,
you who gave yourself to me and made me a mother.

Where is my dowry? I counted it out
on the field you turned over to take the fleece.
That golden ram is my dowry –
though if I asked: 'Restore it', you'd refuse.
My dowry is yourself, alive;
my dowry is your crew.
Go, bastard, compare that to the wealth of Sisyphus!
That you breathe to take wife and be ungrateful,
you owe to me.
Listen well – but wait. Why should I
let you know the price?

Where this rage leads, I will follow.
Perhaps I will repent,
but I repent caring for you.

I leave it for the god who churns my heart.
I do not know what power moves my mind.

XIII: Laodamia to Protesilaus

Laodamia and Protesilaus, queen and king of Phylace, are married and in love. He has set off to fight the Trojan War and she is full of fear. There is a prediction that the first Greek to set foot on Trojan soil will die and she is anxious it will be him. This poem has a distracted, jumpy feel – like a series of half-written letters, getting more fragmented as Laodamia gets increasingly hysterical. It would be full of irony for the Roman audience, who would know that Protesilaus fulfils the prophecy and is killed by Hector.

There are many codas to this story: in one, Laodamia grieves so deeply, Protesilaus is permitted to return to her for three hours – William Wordsworth's poem 'Laodamia' evokes this scene. In another, Laodamia becomes obsessed with a statue of Protesilaus, constantly holding and kissing it. When her father throws it in the fire she jumps in too.

¶

My loving heart sends a hello. I hope you're healthy.
I hope this reaches my husband.

Reports say you're held at Aulis by the wind.
Where was that wind when you left me?
I wished the seas would rise to stop your oars –
I wished for floods.
I could have given you more kisses and requests –
there are so many things I want to say.

But you were swept
by the wind sailors long for,
that breaks lovers' hearts.

I loosed myself from your arms, Protesilaus,
all half unsaid,
hardly time for a sad 'farewell.'
The north wind swooped, seized and stretched your sails.
For as long as I could see you I followed
your eyes with my eyes, and when I couldn't see you
I could see your sails and I followed your sails
with my eyes, until I couldn't see you or sails,
nothing but sea,
and the light left with you,
dark bloomed, my blood retreated,
knees failed, I sank – they say –
to the floor.

Your father and my parents, horrified,
threw freezing water on me,
which was well-meant, but useless.
I didn't want my desolate life.

Consciousness crept back, and pain.
Love has rent my heart.
I'm careless about my hair,

and there's no fun in shiny clothes.
Like Bacchus' drunks, I go hither
and thither, where the mad go.

The matrons of Phylace gather, shouting:
'Put on your royal robes, Laodamia!'
But is it right to wear cloth dyed costly colours,
whilst my husband wars in Troy?
Am I to comb my hair, while you wear a helmet?
Model new skirts, while you wear armour?
In my dowdy dress they'll say I try to be like you;
I'll pass days solemnly.

* * *

Dangerous Paris – dashing, cruel –
may you be as poor an enemy as you were a guest.
If only your hostess had found you ugly,
or taken no pleasure in your face.
And you, Menelaus, miss Helen too much –
how many tears will fall for your revenge?
Gods, keep us from evil,
let my beloved praise Jove for a safe return!

But I'm frightened – this damned war –
tears flow like snow-melt.
Ilion and Tenedos and Simois and Xanthus and Ida –
even the names scare me.

Would he have dared the theft, if he didn't have the power?
He knew his strength.
He arrived, dressed up in gold,
with Phrygian wealth on his person,
potent men and ships –
and were these just a fraction?
They were the bait for Helen, Leda's daughter,
will they also bring us grief?

I fear the one called 'Hector.'
If I'm dear to you, beware,

be mindful, keep his name in your heart,
and when you've avoided him,
avoid the others:
there are so many Hectors.

When you prepare for battle, say:
'Laodamia needs me spared.'
If Troy's fate is to fall,
let it fall with you unscarred.
Let Menelaus struggle, press to meet his enemy –
a husband must find his stolen wife.
You are different: fight to live,
return to your queen.

Please, Trojans, let one go out of so many –
blood would empty my body.
He's not the type of man who bares steel in the shock of war
or rushes savagely at enemies,
he's better at love.
Let others kill and let him love.

*   *   *

I confess, my soul strove to call you back,
but I feared an evil auspice.
There was already one – leaving your father's house,
to go to Troy, you stumbled at his door.
I moaned inside, and in my secret heart thought:
may this be a good omen instead.
I tell you now, in case you're too keen with your arms.
I hope my fears dry up.

There is a prophecy, too, marking one man –
the first to step on Trojan land.
Unhappy wife, to be the first widow!
May the gods stop you being too eager –
of the thousand ships, let yours be the thousandth ship,
the last to ride the spent wave.
Let me say this too: don't hurry
or only hurry home
speeding with oar and sail to here.

It doesn't matter if it's clouded or bright
you are my day's terror, then come to me at night –
when I stroke myself, pretend
it's your hand; lure sleep with lies.
In my sorrow, I gasp at ghosts.

But why's your face so pale?
Why do your lips seem to lament?
I shake slumber and pray to night spirits.
Every altar's foggy with my incense.
I offer incense, and teardrops brighten it
as wine drops brighten it.

When shall I fold you in my arms, safe, returned;
submerge myself in bliss?
When will I have you lying by me on the couch,
telling tales of war?
And whilst you tell me, though I'll love to hear,
you'll snatch kisses and get them back.
The words of well-told tales meet pauses like this –
they refresh the teller's mouth...

But then Troy looms –
hope rots to fear.
This, too, scares me: that the sea forbids you move
yet you make ready,
defy the wind that's saying no.
You trim sail to leave,
though Neptune's closed his kingdom.
Come home!
It is not fluke but god himself delays you.
What is the quest of this vast war but some wanton whore?
Ships: reverse while you can!

But what am I doing? Do I call you back?
It is unlucky – I wish you calm seas, caressing gales...

*   *   *

I envy Trojan women
who see the fates of those they love.
There each new bride straightens her husband's helmet
puts his sword into his hand and receives a kiss –
a task delicious to both –
leads him outside, tells him to come back,
makes sure he's given Jove his offerings.
With her words new in his mind
he thinks of home and fights more cautiously.
At night she strips off his shield, unlooses his head,
comforts his weary body.
But we are uncertain,
fearing all things that could be...

*　　*　　*

Whilst you fight in another place
I have made a waxen doll, so I don't forget your face.
I will stroke it and hold it
I will tell it words of love.
Believe me, it's uncanny.
It could be you, Protesilaus, if it talked to me!
I hold it close like a husband and tell it my sorrow,
as if it can reply.

*　　*　　*

By your return and you, who are my god,
by the fire of love and our wedding day,
I will come to be with you, wherever you call from – whether
you live, whether everything I fear happening happens...

The letters end now. I'll nag you one last time!
If you care for me, care for yourself.

XIV: Hypermestra to Lynceus

Belus has twin sons, Danaus and Aegyptus, and divides his kingdom between them, giving Libya to Danaus and Arabia to Aegyptus. Danaus has fifty daughters, also known as the Danaides. His twin brother, Aegyptus, has fifty sons. Aegyptus suggests to Danaus that their sons and daughters should marry. Suspecting this to be a plot to strip him of his half of the kingdom, Danaus agrees; but on the wedding night, when the sons are all drunk, he gives each of his daughters a knife to murder their grooms.

Hypermestra is the only daughter who spares her new husband, instead helping Lynceus to escape. She is discovered and at the time of this letter is imprisoned.

There is a strange diversion in this narrative when Hypermestra thinks about her ancestor, the priestess Io, who caught the attention of Jupiter. He began to come to her at night, making his wife Juno so angry she turned Io into a cow. It perhaps occurs as an image of another woman's destiny twisted cruelly by desires other than her own.

As a postscript in some versions, the Danaides are punished in the underworld by having to carry water in jugs with holes in them.

¶

I send this letter to the one surviving brother –
the rest lie murdered by their brides.
Because I was faithful, I'm prisoner in the palace,
oppressed by chains.
My hand shrank from piercing your throat – this is my crime.
They'd have praised a killer.
But better to be charged than please my father;
my hands are clean.

There were torches at our marriage.
May my father scar me with their flame, char my face,
shove his sword through my neck,
deal death meant for my husband –
I won't repent:
the faithful never repent faith.
Let Danaus and my cruel sisters say sorry,
they're the evil ones.

I'm dazed, remembering that unholy night;
trembling fetters my hand.
You think your wife would have the nerve to kill?
I can't even write of others' crimes.

And yet I'll try: dusk descended,
it was the end of day, the start of night.
We fifty Danaides entered the hall.
Aegyptus, our uncle, welcomed brides for his sons.

On every side burnished lamps
and altar-fires spluttered with profanity.
The crowd chanted: 'Hymen Hymenaeus!'
but the gods shunned us that day.

Fifty grooms, confused by wine, joyous,
fresh flowers in their sweaty hair,
burst into bridal chambers – their tombs –

to press beds that would be graves.
And then, heavy with meat and booze, they slept.
A thick silence covered Argos.

And then I thought I heard the screams of dying men –
no, I *did* hear. My fear was true.
Blood retreated. Heat left my limbs, my soul –
I was frozen to my newlyweds' bed.

As slender ears of corn convulse in breeze,
as winter's breeze churns poplar leaves,
so I trembled – or more –
whilst you slept (I'd slipped you sleeping pills.)

But my father's outlawed fear –
I stood and clutched the sword.
I will not lie – three times I raised it,
three times it slumped again.
Let me confess: it traced your throat,
but fear and tenderness
kept me from daring the thrust.
My hand refused.

I ripped my clothes, shredded my hair,
muttered:
'Your father is strict, Hypermestra. Perform
his command, let this one join his brothers.
But I'm young, I'm gentle,
these tender hands aren't used to weapons.
Have guts like your sisters, they've probably
slain their husbands by now!
If this hand could deal death,
it would be bloody with my death.
They must die for seizing their uncle's realms –
leaving us exiled with our old father!
Yet even if they deserve this –
why do we deserve this?
Why should I spoil my innocence? What are swords to me?
I'd rather the spindle.'

So I argued with myself. Tears
followed words as I looked at your body.
You tossed, groped for my embrace –
almost sliced your hand on the blade.
I feared my father, my father's minions, the dawn.
I woke you:
'Get up, you're the only brother left!
This night will never end unless you hurry.'
You jerked in terror, sleep's dullness gone,
saw the sword in my girl's hand.
When you asked me why, I answered: 'Go, while night allows.'
You fled and I remained.

Early that morning, Danaus counted his dead son-in-laws.
He saw the crime was incomplete.
He took it badly –
too little blood had been poured.
I was yanked by the hair and dragged into this jail
as my reward.

Juno loathes our line – think of the time
her wrath transformed Io to a heifer.
The mooing was sufficient punishment,
as she could not keep Jove's love.
From the banks of the stream the new cow
saw her strange skull.
Trying to complain, she lowed –
terrified by her shape, her voice.
Why rage, unhappy girl? Why gaze at yourself
in water's shadows? Why count your feet?
Juno dreaded you as a rival for Jove,
but now you hunger for green and grass;
you stoop to drink at the spring
and fear impaling yourself.
Once you were rich – rich enough for a god –
now you're bare on bare ground.
You cross oceans and land,
welcomed by kindred streams.
Why wander long seas?

You cannot fly from yourself.
You are hunter and hunted –
escaping, chasing...

The Nile, with its seven mouths,
stripped that maddened beast from her body.
But why talk of far-off things, dusty tales?
I have my own sad story.

My father and uncle are at war,
we are driven from our home to the edges of earth.
Aegyptus has full power as king,
whilst we are exiles, wandering.
You are the only one of fifty brothers left,
I weep for the dead and the bringers of death.
I have lost as many sisters as you have brothers;
mourn all of them.

Because you live, I will be tortured.
When the admirable accused are punished
for purity, what must the guilty suffer?
There were a hundred of us, now there are two.

Lynceus, be worthy of the gift:
help me,
or abandon me to death, but if I die
bury my body in secret,
wet my bones with tears.
Have my sepulchre engraved with this epitaph:
'Exiled Hypermestra paid an unfair price,
and died to save her cousin.'

I'd write more, but the chains hurt my wrists,
and fear has taken my strength.

XV: Sappho to Phaon

This letter stands out from the others – a historical dramatic mono-
logue rather than a mythical one, whose central figure occupies a
very different world from that of Ovid's goddesses and queens.
Sappho was a lyric poet born about 613 BC in Sicily who spent
her adult life on Lesbos, and in this poem her lover Phaon is a
simple boatman. Although Sappho was known for her passionate
relationships with girls, she was also thought to have had a husband,
Cercylas, with whom she had a daughter. There is also a reference
here to her brother Charaxus, who disappointed her by becoming
involved with a prostitute.

Sappho is said to have written nine books of lyric poetry, but
only one complete poem of hers has survived – the rest are frag-
ments. Because of this every generation of readers in some way
invents Sappho, imagining a whole from the pieces. Ovid's Sappho
is not the Sappho of modern readers, who may find the voice of
this poem surprising – ageing, sexually boastful and foolish, it goes
against the grain on the delicate, intelligent voice recent translators
of Sappho's work such as Anne Carson have conjured. However,
in many ways Ovid seems to have created the voice of this sensual
lyric poet by drawing on his own experience, and the two poets
do share a vision of the world in which love is central. Fragment
16 in Carson's translation begins with a statement we can imagine
on the lips of any of Ovid's *Heroines*:

> Some men say an army of horse and some men say an army on foot
> and some men say an army of ships is the most beautiful thing
> on the black earth. But I say it is
> > what you love.

¶

Tell me, when you saw this writing,
did you recognise the hand's shapes –
or did you ask who the author was
until you read the signature *Sappho?*

Perhaps you wonder why my lines vary in length
when I'm known for lyrics
but I weep for love and the elegy's for weeping.
Lyres don't accompany tears.

I burn as stubbled acres burn, as harvests lit
when wild east-winds urge surging flame.
You live by Etna, Phaon –
fire eats in me, molten as Etna's fire.

I can't sing songs for strings –
they're for careless minds.
I can't find charm in Phyrrha's girls
or any other Lesbian.

Glittering Cydro is nothing.
There's no pleasure in gazing
at the hundred women I've bedded in sin
when my lust's yours, not theirs.

You're beautiful. You're young and hungry.
You ambushed my eyes.
Pick up the bow, pose as Apollo –
with horns you could be Bacchus.

Apollo loved Daphne, Bacchus a maid,
and neither wrote poems.
Muses slip such seductive words to me,
my name's known round the earth

and even the singer Alcaeus
isn't praised more –
if I'm denied beauty, weigh beauty
against my genius.

If I'm small, my name fills the land –
measure my name for my real height.
If I'm not dazzlingly pale, recall Andromeda –
fair to Perseus, though a swarthy foreigner.

Besides, white pigeons mate with grey,
turtle-doves fuck emerald parrots.
If none can be yours until they're worthy,
none can be yours.

When you saw my verses I seemed beautiful enough.
You said it was a kind of grace.
I'd recite them (lovers remember such things)
whilst you stole kisses.

You liked this too. I pleased in every way.
Pleased most when we made love:
you thrilled to playfulness,
quick rhythms, teasing words

then our lives mingled, voluptuous,
flesh swooned to languid languor.
Now you prey on girls in Sicily.
What's Lesbos to my envy?

Send him back
Sicilian mothers and daughters!
Don't be tricked by his fictions; the fawning tongue
that tells you what he told me.

You too, Erycina of Sicily's mountains –
I'm yours, protect your poet!
Must my ill luck persist
all the bitter way?

At six, I hugged my father's bones;
they suckled on my tears.
My brother, blistered by a harlot,
suffered loss and stinking shame,

degraded, he roams grey-green seas,
chasing wealth he wasted.
As I scolded him, he hates me –
that's the truth-teller's reward.

And as if there was a lack of things to drain me,
there's my tiny daughter
and you: last cause of my complaint.
It is a perfect storm that whips my craft.

Look: hair tangles round my throat,
my fingers are naked,
my dress is threadbare, no gold
or Arabian scent laces my hair.

For whom should I preen or try to please?
The reason I got dressed is gone.
My heart's pierced by the slightest shaft,
there's always cause to always be in love.

Did the Fates decide this at my birth?
Spin my life with a mean strand?
Or does craving become character?
Light verse softened my nature.

Why be surprised I'm taken by that first fuzz of hair
on youths who move men's' loins?
I feared Aurora might steal him but Cephalus,
her first prey, still holds her eye.

The moon's huge eye should see him –
she would keep him asleep.
Venus would have him in heaven
but she knows even Mars would be charmed.

O neither man or boy, a lovely age,
you are exquisite, you are splendid.
Come here, pretty one, sink in these arms,
I don't need love but let yourself be loved.

As I write a tear appears like a dewdrop –
see how many blot this spot.
If you had to go you could have gone gently,
could have said goodbye.

You didn't take my tears or kisses.
I didn't even get to dread the hurt.
You have left nothing, nothing but this ache
and took nothing to remind you.

I asked nothing, not that I would've asked
except to ask: forget nothing.
By our love – may it not leave –
by my nine goddesses,

I swear, when someone said: 'Your boy's gone'
I couldn't cry or speak.
Words forsook my tongue, dust-eyed,
I was paralysed.

Then grief caught and I struck myself,
clutched fists of hair and keened
like a mother whose son is dead, heaving
his carcass on the pyre.

My brother swells with my sorrow,
he passes my eyes again, again,
making my grief seem sordid, saying:
'Why do you howl when your daughter lives?'

Shame and love don't fit:
everyone's watching, but I still expose myself.
Phaon, my love, the dreams that bring you back
are more vivid than the day or day's beauty.

Across space and time, I find you
but then sleep's not long enough.
Often my neck seems to crush your arms
or I feel your neck in my arms

or I recognise that circling tongue, those kisses
you demanded and gave up
and as I fondle you, lips utter words that seem
like waking truth; shelter what seems.

I flush to tell you further, but it all happens –
the rapture...the wetness... I'm lawless...
But then the sun bleaches the earth,
I groan as sleep goes.

I make for groves and grottos
as if they could help, delirious
as if at Enyo's ghastly touch,
hair slack around my throat,

past caverns, blades of hanging rock
lovely as marble once.
I find woods where we once lay,
thick shade I thought our quilt.

But the forest's filled with absence –
without you it's tawdry:
our pressed-down blades,
sod hollowed by our weight.

I lie stroking a flower-deep indent,
water the grasses with tears
where branches have laid down leaves,
and there's no birdsong,

only the nightingale, mournful mother
lamenting Itys, singing 'Itys'
as Sappho sings 'lost love' –
nothing else but night's hush

and a spring, bright and transparent,
where some think spirits live,
water-lotus spread above it
and the earth tender with moss

where I've flattened tired limbs
and heard a Naiad whisper:
'Since you waste with unrequited love,
you must seek Ambracia.

There sun stares at the waters
and one man, ablaze with love,
hurled himself smack
down into sea unharmed

and at once felt passion gone,
love gone, pain gone.
This is the place's power. Go now:
seek rocks, don't fear the fall.'

With this she ceased and vanished. Scared,
I rose with filling eyes.
I'll go and find the rock described.
No fear: hysteria drives it out.

Whatever will be will be better than this.
Air will bear this slight body.
Let love soften the drop, let death
not come from blameless waves.

I'll dedicate my tortoise-shell lyre
to the sun as we both love its sound.
But why send me lonely to those shores
when you could turn around?

You can help more:
in radiance and warmth can be my sun.
If I perish by your sadism, worse than the sea's,
can you endure being the cause?

I'd rather press my breast to yours
than hurl it into sky –
the breasts, Phaon, that you admired,
when you thought me talented.

Where's eloquence now?
Grief halts the mouth I had.
For grief, music won't come:
my plectrum's dumb, my lyre is dumb.

Daughters of Lesbia, fiancées and wives
whose names have been sung to my lyre,
all you women who've made me notorious,
stop baying for my songs.

Phaon has swept away all you loved –
pathetic, how I almost said *my Phaon!*
If he returns so will the singer,
my powers are plucked away.

Zephyrs catch my words, would catch
your sails, my lazy boy, if you could feel.
If you lay charms on your stern, if you mean
to return why destroy me with delays?

Lift anchor! Venus clears the sea
for lovers, winds will speed your way,
Cupid control the tiller, delicate
fingers spreading and furling the sail.

But if you want to get far away from me –
though there's no reason to run away from me –
write to let me know my loss
so I might find my fate in water.

Glossary of names

Absyrtus	Medea's brother
Achelous	a river god
Achilles	Greek hero of the Trojan wars, central to Homer's *Iliad*
Adonis	a boy loved by Venus
Aeëtes	king of Colchis; father of Medea
Aegisthus	Clytemnestra's lover and accomplice in the murder of her husband, Agamemnon
Aegeus	king of Athens; father of Theseus
Aegyptus	son of Belus and twin brother of Danaus; he has fifty sons
Aeneas	a Trojan; son of Anchises and Aphrodite; by the time of Virgil his story had been altered to include a prophecy that he would be founder of Rome
Aeolus	god of the winds
Aethra	mother of Theseus
Agamemnon	king of Mycenae, brother of Menelaus, father to Orestes; leader of Greeks at Troy
Agrius	Deianara's uncle; Oeneus' brother
Ajax	cousin of Achilles
Alcaeus	a lyric poet and contemporary of Sappho
Androgeos	son of Minos and Pasphaë, older brother of Ariadne, who dies trying to kill a wild bull – Minos suspects Aegeus has arranged it so declares war on Athens
Andromache	wife of Hector
Andromeda	an Ethiopian Princess chained to a rock by her father to appease a monster; Perseus rescues her
Antilochus	son of Nestor and Eurydice; one of the bravest Greeks in the Trojan War
Apollo	the sun-god
Aquilo	the north wind
Ariadne	daughter of the King of Crete, Minos, and his wife Pasiphaë; half-sister of the Minotaur
Atlas	a Titan who holds up the celestial sphere
Aurora	goddess of dawn
Bacchus	god of wine

Belus	father of the twin brothers Danaus and Aegyptus
Briseis	daughter of the King of Lyrnessus; after her family and husband are killed by Achilles she becomes his concubine
Busiris	a king of Egypt killed by Hercules
Canace	daughter of Aeolus; sister of Macareus with whom she commits incest
Cassandra	daughter of Trojan king Priam; she is fated to predict the future but be ignored
Cephalus	Ovid blends two characters with this name: a king of Athens with a spear that never misses its target, and the son of Hermes, abducted by the goddess Aurora
Cerberus	dog that guards the underworld
Clytemnestra	wife of Agamemnon; mother of Orestes, Iphigenia and Electra; she plots the murder of her husband with her lover, Aegisthus, after Agamemnon has sacrificed Iphigenia to appease the goddess Artemis
Creon	Creusa's father; ruler of Ephyre
Creusa	daughter of Creon; Jason leaves Medea to marry her
Cydro	a companion of Sappho
Danaus	son of Belus and twin brother of Aegyptus, he has fifty daughters known as the Danaides
Daphne	a nymph who rejected all men
Deianira	wife of Hercules
Deiphobus	a son of Priam
Demaphoon	the son of Theseus and Phaedra
Diana	goddess of the hunt, sister of Apollo
Dido	founder of Carthage
Diomedes	a barbarous king of Thrace, who owns four mares so terrifying they eat human flesh
Enyo	a goddess of war who often accompanies Mars into battle
Erycina	an area in Sicily, but also a term of address used for Venus
Europa	daughter of the Phoenician king Agenor
Eurus	the east wind
Faunus	the Roman version of the Greek god Pan; deity of woods, fields and fecundity

Furies	avenging spirits who punished those who injure their own kin
Geryon	a man with three heads who had a herd of amazing cattle which Hercules stole before killing him
Hecate	goddess associated with the underworld, the moon and witchcraft
Hector	eldest son of Priam and Hecuba, a leader of the Trojan army
Hecuba	wife of Priam
Helen	daughter of Jove and Leda and a great beauty; wife of Menelaus and mother of Hermione, she is abducted by Paris in an act that starts the Trojan War
Hercules	son of Jove and Alcmene
Hermione	daughter of Helen and Menelaus – she is promised first to Orestes and then to Pyrrhus
Hippodamia	mother of Atreus, Thyrestes and Pittheus
Hippolytus	the son of Theseus and his Amazonian lover Hippolyte; stepson of Phaedra
Hydra	snake with many heads killed by Hercules
Hymen	god of marriage
Hypermestra	one of the fifty daughters of Danaus
Hypsipyle	queen of Lemnos
Io	a priestess Jove fell in love with, who was turned into a cow
Iole	daughter of Iardanus, taken by Hercules as a concubine as part of the spoils of victory
Iulus	son of Aeneas
Jason	son of Aeson; known for his quest for the golden fleece on a ship called the *Argo*, with his Argonauts
Jove	the highest god (Jupiter to the Greeks), he raped Leda, disguised as a swan, fathering Helen
Juno	wife and sister of Jove
Laodamia	wife of Protesilaus the king of Phylace
Leda	mother of Helen, Clytemnestra, Castor and Pollux
Lucina	goddess of childbirth
Lynceus	one of the fifty sons of Aegyptus; husband of Hypermestra
Macareus	son of Aeolus; brother of Canace
Mars	god of war, son of Jove and Juno

Medea	one of the daughters of Aeëtes, king of Colchis; a priestess of Hecate; sister of Absyrtus
Menelaus	son of Atreus, brother of Agamemnon and husband of Helen
Minerva	goddess of art and science, daughter of Jove
Minos	king of Crete
Minotaur	the offspring of Pasiphaë and a bull; Ariadne's half-brother
Naiad	kind of freshwater nymph
Neptune	god of the sea, brother of Jove
Nessus	centaur killed by Hercules
Notus	the south wind
Oenone	daughter of a river-god, who lives on the slopes of Mount Ida
Oeneus	father of Deianira
Omphale	queen of Lydia
Orestes	son of Agamemnon and Clytemnestra
Paris	son of the king of Troy, Priam
Patroclus	attendant and close friend of Achilles
Pasiphaë	wife of Minos; mother of Androgeos, Ariadne, Phaedra and the Minotaur (with a bull)
Pelias	king of Iolcus; his daughters were induced to kill their father by Medea, who told them it would restore him to youth
Peleus	son of Aeacus, father of Achilles
Pelops	son of Tantalus; descendant of Jove
Penelope	daughter of the king of Sparta; wife of Ulysses
Perseus	from Argos; rescuer of Andromeda
Phaedra	daughter of Minos and Pasiphaë; wife of Theseus and so stepmother to Hippolytus
Phaon	name given to the lover of Sappho in classical literature
Phoebe	Helen's sister-in-law; Hermione's aunt
Phoenix	the son of Amyntor, an eminent Greek
Phyllis	daughter of a Thracian king
Polydamus	a close friend of Hector, known for his wise advice
Priam	king of Troy; father of Hector, Cassandra and Paris
Protesilaus	king of Phylace; husband of Laodamia
Pyrrhus	the son of Achilles by Deidamia

Sappho	the lyric poet born in 613 BC in Sicily who spent her adult life on Lesbos
Scylla	a sea-monster
Sisyphus	a king of Corinth – Creon would have inherited his wealth
Sychaeus	Dido's first husband, murdered by her brother
Tantalus	son of Jove, father of Pelops and Niobe
Telemachus	son of Penelope and Ulysses
Theseus	son of Aegeus, the Athenian king
Tyndareus	king of Sparta; father of Helen; grandfather of Hermione
Ulysses	the son of Laertes, king of Ithaca, known for his cunning and trickery
Venus	goddess of love, daughter of Jove and Dione
Zephyr	the west wind

Further Reading

The three versions of *Heroides* I referred to during the writing of this book are:

Ovid: Heroides and Amores, translated Grant Showerman (Loeb Classical Library, William Heinemann, 1931)
Ovid: Heroides, translated Harold Cannon (E.P. Dutton & Co, 1971)
Ovid: Heroides, translated Harold Isbell (Penguin, 1990)

Other Ovid translations I found particularly inspiring were:

Ted Hughes: *Tales from Ovid* (Faber and Faber, 2002)
Ovid: *The Art of Love*, translated by James Michie (Modern Library, 2002)

The critical texts on *Heroides* I found most useful, aside from Harold Isbell's notes, were:

Howard Jacobson: *Ovid's Heroides* (Princeton University Press, 1974)
Florence Verducci: *Ovid's Toyshop of the Heart* (Princeton University Press, 1985)

For further insight into Ovid's sources I would highly recommend:

Homer: *The Iliad*, translated Richard Lattimore (Harper & Row, 1967)
Homer: *The Odyssey*, translated Richard Lattimore (University of Chicago Press, 1951)
Virgil: *The Aeneid*, translated Frederick Ahl (Oxford University Press, 2007)
Robert Graves: *The Greek Myths*, complete edition (Penguin, 1992)

www.ingramcontent.com/pod-product-compliance
Lightning Source LLC
Jackson TN
JSHW080853211224
75817JS00002B/24